Praise for
Wake Up! Your Life Is Calling

"That rare combination of the inspirational story that has both a message and a road-map to where you want your life to be. This powerful life parable enables you to walk in the shoes of someone who has been on the path. Mike provides the empowerment . . . all readers have to do is follow the process. Change is not easy, impossible without a Sherpa. Mike is a master guide!"

~Stewart Levine, Esq., author of *Getting to Resolution,*
The Book of Agreement, and *Collaborate 2.0*

"Mike Jaffe is a great friend and wrote an amazing book! Read it, take the action, and love your new you."

~Sandy Vilas, Master Certified Coach, Chief Executive Officer,
Coach U, Inc.

"9/11 set off a quickening of human evolution that has resulted in the status quo no longer being good enough for millions of people. Mike Jaffe is a shining example of that and he has written an impactful guide for anyone feeling the urge to change but who is not sure how. Live his story and you'll be rewriting your own."

~Laura Berman Fortgang, Coaching pioneer, Author of
Now What? 90 Days to a New Life Direction

"Filled with useful tips and insights; you'll go back to it over and over, gaining new insights each time."

~Laura Rose, Corporate Exit Strategist, Rose Coaching, and
Author of *TimePeace: Making Peace With Time*

"Mike Jaffe is the real deal. He has directly experienced one of the worst traumas of our history and transformed his life completely because of it. *Wake Up!* is full of hard-earned insights, revelations, and suggested shifts in thought and behavior that, if acted upon, can indeed change your life for the better. Highly recommended for those who desire to live life to the fullest."

~Kathy Caprino, M.A., President, Ellia Communications, and Author of *Breakdown Breakthrough*

"Ready to move from fine to something truly outstanding? This book will absolutely take you there. Mike will take you through a journey that will open your eyes wide to the reasons why we settle and provide you with the tools you need to make your life extraordinary. A must-read for anyone who knows they want more."

~Angela Nielsen, Founder and Creative Director, One Lily Creative Agency

"*Wake Up! Your Life is Calling* is a great read and a wonderful resource for those who want to start living and be the person they were meant to be. Change is not easy for anyone, and your tools for change make it doable and achievable for those who are ready to do something different in their lives."

~Deborah Brown-Volkman, Professional Certified Coach; Career, Life, and Mentor Coach; and President, Surpass Your Dreams, Inc.

"Mike's experiences and how he dealt with his storms are powerful reminders of what's possible for us all. This book is a great wake up call."

~Robert Herzog, Founder & CEO, ZogSports

"*Wake Up!* is an exceptional book. It is a powerful call to action that resonates with ideas that are easily transferable to individuals and companies of any size. Jaffe provides powerful insight to guide the reader through the journey with personal accountability. An immensely enjoyable and valuable read for anyone seeking sage advice in navigating today's rapidly changing world."

~Nancy Newman, Vice President, Sales Communications & Training, Fortune 500 Company

Is This Book for You?

Over the years I've worked with countless people to define their moments of truth, helping them *wake up* to new possibilities.

Is there a part of you that is craving to wake up? And maybe another part that might be hesitant to do so?

Sometimes we succumb to the illusion that we have little control over our lives. Yet, small actions can make big differences. Do you fully realize that life is a gift and that every single day counts? That you don't have endless tomorrows and that the "someday" you are waiting for may never come?

Do You Need a Wakeup Call?

Wakeup call (wᵃk ̍ ŭp ̍): A powerful experience or portentous event that is interpreted as a sign that a major change is needed in the way somebody lives or conducts business

---

If you are wondering whether this book is right for you, ask yourself the following questions:

- Are things in your life just "okay" even though you know there's a lot more that's possible?
- Do you have the courage required to accept that "fine" is not nearly enough?
- Are you facing a big task, a new role, or a different direction?
- Are you seeking a trusted and objective confidante to be a sounding board, push your creativity and limits, and support you in taking the necessary steps?
- Are you letting yourself off the hook too easily—stuck in your old, familiar, and comfortable patterns and ways?

- Do you need someone to help you get out of your own way and hold you accountable so you can play a bigger game and perform at a higher level?
- Are you fearful that the disruption will be too high—that you'll lose everything you've worked so hard to gain?
- Have you considered the true cost of *not* moving forward?

It's not hard to feel like you've lost your direction—or to feel trapped in your current situation—even though you hope that there is a better path out there for your life.

Well, there is! It simply requires courage, vision, and direction to get started on the journey.

Something has to change for you to gain the life you really want so the question really is, are you ready to own it? If so, this book is for you.

What's In It For You

Wondering what you'll gain if you read this book? By reading it, you will:

- stop settling for "fine"
- find a place to begin even if you don't know specifically where you will end up
- feel more confident in your direction
- discover what that "more" is so your life can feel more fulfilled, not "one day" but today
- explore new worlds that you don't even know exist—with these new discoveries will come unlimited new possibilities.

It's time to stop floating or drifting. It's time to stop waiting for "someday." It's time to own your path and start moving powerfully toward what you want. Today is that day. Tomorrow begins today . . .

Wake Up!
Your Life Is Calling

WAKE UP!
Your Life Is Calling

Why Settle for "Fine" When So Much More Is Possible?

MIKE JAFFE

authorHOUSE®

AuthorHouse™
1663 Liberty Drive
Bloomington, IN 47403
www.authorhouse.com
Phone: 1-800-839-8640

First published by AuthorHouse   11/11/2011

ISBN: 978-1-4670-6451-4 (sc)
ISBN: 978-1-4670-6453-8 (hc)
ISBN: 978-1-4670-6452-1 (ebk)

Library of Congress Control Number: 2011918543

Printed in the United States of America

Cover design by Jerry Dorris (jerry@style-matters.com)

This book is printed on acid-free paper.

In the writing of this book, we have changed the names and occupations of all of our personal clients in order to maintain their anonymity.

Contents

PERSIST

CONCLUSION

Dedication

In dedication to my lost colleagues and friends, and to all others who perished on 9/11 or as a result of that day. You are always in my thoughts and you are the flame that helps illuminate my path. Semper Unitas. In recognition, too, of all of those who lost someone special on 9/11 and all others who were personally affected by that event—we are all survivors. This book is for you.

This book stems from an event that is considered one of America's worst days.

The events that changed the world—the tragic events of 9/11—happened more than a decade ago. When they occurred, they gave the United States and the World a wakeup call. The rules had changed. No longer could we take for granted the simple, even comforting, unconscious routine of going to the office and doing our work.

That day was a great equalizer. It didn't matter where you were from, what you did, or what the great plans you had for your life included—if you were up there, it didn't matter.

That day showed how ugly people can be to one another. But rather than focus solely on the tremendous losses we experienced on that day, can we carve out just a little room to also acknowledge the display of how loving, caring, and considerate people were? So many came together in the aftermath of those events, helping one another, sharing water, supplies, and even oxygen in the midst of the toxic cloud, volunteering thousands of hours of their time, donating more blood than the hospitals could store, providing emotional support for those that needed it most, coming together as a town, city, region, country . . . as one community standing together.

It was the end of innocence, yet the creation of possibility.

In the two weeks that followed September 11th, the universe was filled with both loss and possibility. I remember how it felt to be back in the city in the days after 9/11 and how everyone had an unwritten agreement that we would all take care of each other and that we would get through this. Nobody had to say anything—we all said it with our eyes. And we all looked deep into each other in those days; whether stranger or friend, we were all one. The heroism, the warmth, the love, and the support were something I will never forget.

A few months after 9/11, a comedian made a joke regarding the event. However, it became immediately clear how personally sensitive everyone remained regarding that subject as they shouted "too soon!" at the performer. With such a personal and sensitive topic, how can I boldly and confidently declare that even with all of the loss and pain experienced, some good arose from such an event? Is nine, ten, or eleven years later still "too soon"? Will it ever be the appropriate time to make such a declaration?

As you will see from the wisdom contained inside the pages that follow, there is no such thing as the "perfect" time that will satisfy all. As we slowly realize the inevitability that we can never go back, we must dare to look forward to answer the personal question of "what now?" Never to forget, but instead to ensure we are squeezing as much life out of life as we possibly can.

Additionally, how dare us not to? We must honor the losses we've experienced by creating anew—never to replace them, but to continue generating, building, experiencing, doing, and being. Remember, every one of those who were lost would give anything for the chance to have our worst day.

By acknowledging and sharing the insights I have experienced since that infamous point in time, my goal is to shift some of the focus away from the tremendous sadness and loss of 9/11 and to offer instead the hope of growth, wisdom, and new possibilities that have also occurred in its wake.

The specific context of this book and the lessons within are based on life experiences that began with the events of 9/11 and how these experiences shaped my path from there. Even if you have no direct personal connection to that day or it didn't serve as a catalyst in your life, the lessons within this book still apply.

One of the outcomes I am intending to purvey with this book is for you to understand that with every change comes both loss as well as the opportunity for a new beginning. Always.

Much has happened since September 11th. Much is still to come. We are all survivors, every day. Together, let us honor those whom we lost and embrace the strength and wisdom that that experience has created as we forge ahead toward tomorrow, more resolute and wise, fully realizing that we are different not in spite of that event, but because of it.

Welcome to
the WakeUp Revolution!

*"The first step toward getting somewhere is to decide that you
are not going to stay where you are."*

~J.P. Morgan

Welcome to the WakeUp Revolution! I'm Mike Jaffe and I'll be your
guide on this journey.

On September 11, 2001, the world was changed forever. The
events of that day—and my own personal wakeup call on September
10th—not only prompted me to change careers but also gave me the
internal fire and vision to completely transform my life. I worked on
the 96th floor of the World Trade Center, and I lost many friends and
coworkers that day. There will always be a terrible sadness for me when
looking back on that time. As time passed, it gave me the ability to
look back with a different mindset: I realized that 9/11 was not only a
tragic day, but one of the most significant events of my life. I became
aware of how my very grounding and perspective about life and work
had shifted irreversibly.

It started with the realization of how much time I had let slip by.
I had so much opportunity and promise, but I hadn't had the drive or
the vision to know what I really wanted. I had thought only of what it

would take to actually make a change, without looking at the costs of *not* making a change. With a new sense of intention and conviction, I started exploring and experimenting with different ideas and activities that made a positive impact for me and for others in my life.

As I began to understand these distinctions better, I started applying them to my own life and everything started to shift—not just in my career, but in all dimensions of my life. I had a new sense of empowerment and freedom in my career, and I eventually left my safe, corporate job to start my own coaching and consulting firm. My relationships changed as well. My wife and I eliminated any focus on petty complaints and problems and turned our attention and energy toward the unlimited love and possibility that exists for us. My friendships and acquaintances took on a new, vibrant energy. Even my relationship with my children shifted as I brought this renewed sense of ease and fun to them. Overall, my life went from "fine" to "woohoo!"

I recognized that I was drawing on some simple but powerful beliefs and actions in order to design and live an extraordinary life, and I knew I wanted to share these insights and practical steps with as many people as possible: to enable them to shift their relationships with their own lives and to help them create and realize the vision they have for themselves. Those distinctions are captured within the five sections of this book.

One thing I've learned through my experiences is that sometimes it feels like we have no control over our lives. Yet, small decisions can make big differences. I acknowledge and applaud you for taking that first step and picking up this book. Now comes the hard part! Are you ready to create a life that you will love? Do you have the courage and commitment to get in action and take those small but required steps to get there? The "someday" you are waiting for may never come. You are here, and the time is now!

Moments of Truth

Do you know that feeling inside when you experience a loss, have a near-miss, or even feel the threat of losing something important to you? It almost always causes a shift inside, accompanied with an immediate assessment of your situation and life. You realize in that moment that something has to change, that you're not aligned with your true core values, and that you're not playing up to your potential.

Over time, little by little, as you get sucked back into your day-to-day routine, though, it's easy to add layers on top of those values until you lose sight of the meaning they once held and they lose their power to guide you.

What if you were able to generate those moments of truth at any time without having to experience that loss? What if you could turn it on like a light switch, recreating that sense of urgency, that connection to the values you hold deep within, and that sense of accountability and power that accompanies it when you are in a peak state of mind?

That's what this book can be for you, a tool to help you create your own wakeup calls . . . on demand!

By following the steps in this book, you will be empowered to make conscious choices that enable you to break free of your complacency, limiting beliefs, and inactivity so you can overcome your challenges and live the life you've designed—on your terms. You'll dive into many different dimensions of your life and get clear on your ideal vision for each area. You will also explore many possible paths that will take you there (including those you didn't think possible). You will reconnect with your core values and personal preferences, integrating a plan with your unique situation and timeline.

Together, we'll stretch your mind and goals and get you to start dreaming again.

What Is a Human WakeUp Call?

Chances are, you're here because you want something to change. There are a lot of flavors when it comes to change as well as lots of nuance. For some of you, you're driven by a need to move away from where you are in some aspect of your life, whether it's your work situation, your physical health and well-being (or lack thereof), an unsupportive relationship, or something else that isn't serving you productively. Maybe it feels flat, it might be painful, or perhaps it's just not enough. Recognizing that you're not willing to settle for where you are is such an important step in ultimately taking on the change. This is what I consider a "push" movement. It's moving away from something you no longer want. You may have no idea where you want to go or how to get there. You've simply realized that you can't stay where you are any longer. The costs are starting to outweigh the benefits and comfort of staying put.

For others of you, you're driven by the need or desire to move toward something—a bigger job, a new challenge, the person you've just met who's got your stomach reeling with butterflies. You've had a flash of a vision of what it could be like. Whether it's in full Technicolor clarity or it's still fuzzy, there's some kind of "pull" driving you toward it, and it's strong enough to have caused a shift inside of you.

We'll further define these "push" and "pull" concepts later in the book as we discover how we need both of these forces to work as partners to get us over the rickety bridge of change. In fact, you'll see these concepts show up in many forms throughout the book (and, if you look, throughout your life)!

The Coaching Experience

My goal in this book is to give you a coaching experience as best as I can through the written word. Then, it is your turn to engage and become active. I can ask you questions, offer perspectives, and give you prompts, but real change will only take place if you accept the invitation to see your life differently and to begin making changes. Just as I do in my live coaching practice, I am asking you to take ownership for your life and the change you seek.

Since we are going to engage in a coaching experience in this book, I'd better spend a little more time explaining what coaching really is. The best definition I've heard about coaching is that it is the experience of essentially helping people unlock their potential so they can maximize their performance. I like to substitute the word "experience" for "performance" because I believe that maximizing your experience has more depth and dimension than maximizing your performance, which is typically judged by some external, artificial metric. Your experience includes bringing more passion, energy, and meaning into both your thoughts and your actions, ultimately giving you the confidence to play bigger, which does, indeed, maximize your performance. But it also includes the process of getting there too—not just the outcome.

After all, isn't that what we are ultimately seeking? To squeeze as much life out of life as we can? We can't always control the outcomes or results—there are too many variables outside of our influence at play—but we do have enormous control over our own thoughts and actions. Coaching teaches us how to strengthen our own self-mastery. Master ourselves and we will master our lives.

Tenets of the WakeUp Revolution

What is the philosophy of the WakeUp Revolution? I define it with the following tenets:

- It's realizing that life is a gift, and every single day counts.
- It's looking forward and saying, "What now?" not looking back, saying, "I wish I had."
- It's designing your life the way you want it to be, so life doesn't just "happen" to you.
- It's believing in the possibility of your desired life, not a life of compromises.
- It's remembering what's really important, so you can slow down and breathe again.
- It's having the courage to take small steps now, instead of watching days slip past.

My vision is to have millions of people join the WakeUp Revolution and rewrite their tomorrow so that at the end of their respective journeys, instead of looking back with lament, regret, and sorrow, saying, "If only . . . " or "I wish I had . . . " they can look back and say, "Wow! What a ride!"

For more information on the WakeUp Revolution, visit www.HumanWakeUpCall.com

Are You Ready to Roll up Your Sleeves?

Within this book, you will find sections focusing on the following five key themes—perspective, purpose, play, plan, and persist—which together can help you create the life you want to lead. The chapters within each section will offer you tools, techniques, insights, and suggestions that will direct you through the steps for leveraging each distinction on your way toward designing and creating an extraordinary life for yourself. As you put these tools and techniques to use, you will get better at using them. However, give yourself permission to make some mistakes at first. In fact, if you're not making mistakes, you're not playing fully. Have the courage, get in the game, and make your mistakes. That is how you will grow!

In the first section, *Perspective*, we'll focus on *shifting your mindset*. We'll make it clear why it's so important to climb out of that quicksand known as "things are fine" and create a sense of urgency to own your path fully. We'll challenge your perception of "the truth" and significantly expand the universe of what you believe is possible. In doing so, we're going to disrupt those negative thoughts and patterns that have been holding you back and wake up parts of you that have been dormant, hiding, or playing too small to fully serve you.

Those shifts we just defined are enough to completely transform your life. However, we're not going to stop there because once we clear aside some of the mental obstacles that have been holding you back, we want to keep the momentum going. In the second section, *Purpose*, you will get much more clear about who you are, what you value, and where you want to go. After all, how do you know where to go if you haven't designed a future that's meaningful, that's pulling you forward?

Then it's time to *Play*. In this third section, we take concepts and turn them into experiences, what I call "principles into action." As we create this vision, it's important that you *get in action* on this journey. You will get many benefits from simply reading this book, but the magic—the real transformation of your life—will occur only through your actions. That will be the moment of truth—getting on that path. This is where most of us fall down. It is at this point where *commitment, accountability,* and *support* become crucial ingredients to long-term success.

Rather than having to *know how* beforehand, you're going to *learn how* on the road toward getting there. As one of my mentors, Fern Gorin, says, "to know without doing is not to know."* You'll experience much more freedom as you let go of having to know how ahead of time. In fact, you'll want to keep expanding what you don't know, as well as what you know.

As you further discover where you want to go and why you want to get there (that powerful combination of both push and pull), we'll arrive at section four, *Plan*, where you'll get on that rickety bridge and start moving one step at a time toward your desired goal. As part of your Human WakeUp Call experience, I'll be here to encourage you as you take those steps—to remind you of your values and why you are moving forward—and to help you get clear that turning back is not an option—the cost is just too high. I'm not going to pull you across that deep expanse—you have to own your personal journey. But I will be here as an objective partner in crime, bringing you understanding and no judgment, with energy and perspective to keep you moving forward, even when all you want to do is run back to where you were.

As we continue into section five, *Persist*, you will keep taking step after step—falling down, getting up, and reflecting on the growth spurts you're having from being in motion—and your life will change. We'll continue to "teach you to fish" and help you strengthen your own support network so your growth and the positive change you've caused in your life will be sustainable and perpetual. You'll have the tools necessary to continue to create what you *want* in a beautiful dance with what you really *need* (which is a lot less than most people realize).

---

* Fern Gorin is the Founder and Director of the Life Purpose Institute (www.lifepurposeinstitute.com), an organization that trains people to become extraordinary certified life coaches.

Write, Think, or Hum

To fully utilize the lessons within this book, you will want to have something to write on—a notebook or journal—as you read through these chapters.

For all of the questions we ask within this book, write down the first thing that comes to mind, but also write the second and third things that come to your mind. Peel the onion of your thoughts—get past the top layers into the more thoughtful under-layers. We are aiming to get down to a core we'll never reach. However, it's the ongoing journey to the center that's very illuminating. Write as much as you can, because even the simple act of writing can be freeing and empowering.

If you are adamant about not writing, be a thinker. Contrary to current popular belief, thinking about these questions and working through them in your head *is* doing something. Although, these days, when many of us do sneak some thinking time into our overloaded calendar, we often feel guilty that we aren't actually *doing* anything—that we're just wasting time. Yet, "thinking" is a vital lost art that needs to be resurrected if we are to realize the potential of our lives and live with intention and purpose. It is the opposite of reacting, which seems to have won the grand prize in the emotional-activity pageant. Reacting is what we do most of the time now because we're inundated with invasive technology that keeps us so darn busy. Bottom line—write, think, even hum. I don't care what you do as long as you are focusing some of your attention on what these questions mean *for you*. This is the time to focus on yourself for a change.

Ladies and Gentlemen, Make Sure Your Seatbelts Are Firmly Fastened!

If you feel that you've lost some control over your life, the lessons and steps in this book will help you move your life in a better direction. You may have continued down uninspired paths because you were simply stuck, had no vision of where you wanted to go, or were afraid and uncertain of how to break this powerful spell. But if you can find one thing to change for yourself, one thing that makes you feel more alive, then you must do it. The steps in this book can show you how, but only you can employ the actions to get there. As I tell my clients, it's time to "buckle up" because we're about to go on an amazing ride!

No matter what your priorities are—from being a more effective leader to resurrecting a disengaged team to waking up a part of you that's been dormant for too long, you can, without a doubt, create a far greater impact in business and in life than you have so far. In this book, we'll create that urgency that'll kick you in the ass and shout, "Let's Go!" If you're like many of my clients, that extra kick is just what you've been craving. Maybe you want help in understanding the true costs and benefits of all of your options so you can make the best decision possible for you and your family. In our work together, we'll also poke and push and pound down those things that are in your way and keeping you stuck, as well as loosen the powerful beliefs you've created around them that feel so true. Regardless of your unique situation, together, we're going to create new possibilities for you.

If you're ready to move from *fine* to something truly outstanding, buckle up—this is going to be a great ride. Ready to rock and roll?

PERSPECTIVE

"Every exit is an entrance to somewhere else."
~ Tom Stoppard

1

Today Is Your WakeUp Call!

"The next morning, my wife saw that I was dressed and ready to go. She gave me a surprised look and said, 'I thought you were taking the later train today?' She asked me whether we were still having breakfast together or if she should drive me to the station so I could make my normal train. Little did I know, at that moment, I was standing at the crossroads of my life and my answer to that innocent question would determine whether I lived or died . . ."

~Mike Jaffe

Sometimes it's the small decisions that make the biggest differences in our lives. That was the case on that day in September when I had to make a split-second decision on whether or not I'd keep my promise to my family to have breakfast with them before heading to work. Sounds simple enough, right? Have breakfast with the family. But like so many other Americans, my work routine started early—and that meant no time for breakfast with my wife and one-year-old daughter. Except that day was supposed to be different. I had promised myself that work could wait. And, yet, there I was, all set to go to work early, like normal. If I caught my regular train, I'd be at my office by 8:45 AM.

There is a lot of drama built into that excerpt above. I'm not someone who gets entangled in too much drama, but I included it there for a reason. That statement above is part of the story I share with you below. My story. Of course, I didn't know it at the time, but the small decision I made that day really did determine whether I lived or died.

Defining the WakeUp Call

Before I share that story more fully I want to return to our focus for this book, which is about designing and living an extraordinary life, starting today. For many of us, including me, the ability to accomplish this amazing and worthwhile goal starts with a realization—with a wakeup call. But what does that really mean—a wakeup call?

Wakeup calls occur when you experience an event or have a powerful insight that is significant enough to shake you up and scream, "LIFE'S TOO SHORT! WAKE UP!" They remind us that we don't have endless tomorrows. A wakeup call occurs, as I said in the book's introduction, when you become driven by a need to move away from where you are in some aspect of your life (job, relationship, etc.) or driven by the need or desire to move toward something—a bigger job, a new challenge, or something else compelling.

The definition of a "wakeup call" includes a "portentous event that brings an issue to immediate attention" or "a sign to take action concerning something that was overlooked or neglected." I don't want you to have to wait for a "portentous event" or a sign to realize you've been overlooking or neglecting any part of your life. You bought this book and you're receiving this message today—there's your event and your sign.

Why is it important to recognize your own wakeup call, you ask? I sum it up simply by proclaiming that if there are changes you want to make in your life, and you haven't started on them yet (for whatever "reason"), you are wasting precious time! Don't wait until more time has unnecessarily passed, or it simply becomes too late. Stop empowering the reasons and excuses you are using, no matter how real and valid they feel.

Are you able to step outside of your day-to-day life for a moment and really see what a wakeup call might look like for you? Is what I'm saying resonating with you, or is it just a bunch of words on a page? How does the prospect of a wakeup call feel? For some of you, it is utterly terrifying. For others, it's motivational. For still others, no matter how hard you try, it just isn't real. But I'm telling you that it is very real, and the time is now to take an honest look at your life to decide where you want to make powerful and positive changes for yourself, strengthen your relationships with those you love, and create entirely new relationships with those things that have been stopping you all this time.

We're All Hung Over

I have a theory about how life feels for so many of us these days. I see people who have grown all kinds of electronic appendages to their bodies—cell phones, PDAs, iPods, etc. They can't bear to be away from their gadgets. (I thought technology was supposed to make our lives easier?) "What if I miss something important?" is the general sentiment. Guess what? You *are* missing something important right now. It's called "your life!"

As a result of all of this 24/7 access, information overload, and constant stimulation, so many of us feel "hung over" these days. I don't mean that we drank too much tequila last night (at least I don't *remember* drinking that much tequila last night)! What I mean by "hung over" is that we're OVERworked, OVERstructured, OVERloaded, OVERinformed, OVERstimulated, and OVERwhelmed. Too many of us feel this way. By continuing this mode of operation, we get to keep lots of data and information in our brains and be up-to-the-minute on all news and events, but there is a tremendous cost to living this way: burnout.

Fried, frazzled, irritable, and fatigued. All that information intake, all that meeting of deadlines and timelines and schedules and appointments, and you may just find one day you can't do it anymore. Or maybe the opposite—you won't have the energy needed to do anything about it. You may keep pushing through and find that your physical and mental health really start to suffer. Believe me, I understand the importance of meeting family and work responsibilities, but you also need to recognize when it's all too much or you've gotten off course from the life you really want to live.

The truth is, burning out isn't going to serve you, your family, your clients, or anyone. What we want is to get you living the kind of life that feeds you rather than depletes you.

Where Do You Start? My Story

I was in a rut myself for many years. Prior to becoming a coach, I was unsatisfied with much of the work I was doing for most of my career. Days weren't all horrible—I had plenty of good days too. But they just didn't provide the meaning that I was craving.

My biggest problem was that I had no vision for my life. I didn't know where I wanted to go or even how to begin. So I did what most of us do . . . nothing. But then time started melting away—days became months, which soon added up to years. Back then, I worked in New York City and lived in Connecticut. I was commuting two hours *each way* to work (four hours in total each day), and I hated that I didn't have any time to spend with my wife and one-year-old daughter. This was not the husband or dad I wanted to be. But as the sole breadwinner of the family at the time, I couldn't simply stop working. Although I didn't know what to do, I realized that I had to at least stop "losing" days.

Then, one beautiful afternoon, I was having lunch outside, reflecting on my situation and feeling very stuck. Have you ever felt that way, like you're running in place and you know you want things to change but you don't know what to do about it?

Well, there I was, in that exact state and I didn't know what I could do to change it. The thought of switching to another meaningless job again and trying to recreate my career closer to home was completely overwhelming. I was numb.

But then I had an insight, and a vision popped into my head. It was a picture of me at my kitchen table, having a relaxed and enjoyable breakfast with my wife and daughter. We were all smiling and I was very happy. *That* was the kind of husband and dad I wanted to be—not the one who was tired and cranky each day, kissing my daughter who was sound asleep on the forehead, wondering if she even remembered who I was.

I was determined to create that vision as my reality (was that my sign?), and I decided right then that the very next morning, instead of rushing to the early train as I always did, I would take the later train so that I could have breakfast at home with the two of them. Instead of being at my desk by 8:45 AM as I usually was, I would get there a little bit after nine o'clock. This was not going to be a monumental life change. In fact, it was only a twenty-minute difference in my schedule. But, even so, it would be a nice little start in the right direction.

What happened next was so interesting. As soon as I made that simple little decision, something inside of me shifted. It's hard to pinpoint exactly what, but it literally felt as if I had just taken control of my life back—even from just that one small decision I made. That little break from routine changed *everything*. One of the most important lessons I realized from making that decision was that nothing would change until I changed it. It was clear that I would never *find* the time to spend with my family in the morning. I had to *create* it!

I immediately called my wife and shared my intentions with her; for the rest of that afternoon, I felt "bulletproof." Nothing bothered me—in fact, I felt the best I had for a long time. I even enjoyed the rest of the day at work. My job duties were exactly the same, but because I took back the responsibility and accountability for my life, my relationship to what I was doing changed. (Creating a simple intention can be very powerful, regardless of whether it actually occurs or not!) The resentment I felt for my job eased as I realized that I didn't have to make myself miserable and sabotage my situation! That was essentially what I was doing after all, waiting for someone else to force me to change instead of doing something about it myself. But in declaring that intention, I realized that if I was miserable, I had no one to blame but myself.

That evening, I went to bed with a renewed sense of hope, possibility, and empowerment. I still didn't have direction, but I had made a start at getting into action. Life was good!

The next morning came and I got up and dressed at my normal time, not quite sure whether I was going to stay true to my intention of having breakfast with my family or not. It's funny how powerful habits are, even if you haven't been doing them for very long.

My wife, surprised to see that I was already dressed and ready to go, asked quizzically, "I thought you were taking the later train today?" She asked me whether we were still having breakfast together or if she should drive me to the station so I could make my normal train.

The chatter in my head started. "Do I just take the early train and have breakfast together another day? It's just breakfast. We can do it anytime. Will my daughter even be aware that we're having breakfast? Do I risk going in late? Will I get in trouble at work? I've only been there a few months, can I even do this?" Little did I know, at that moment, I was standing at the crossroads of my life. My answer to that innocent question would literally determine my fate.

I always thought I would see the most important day of my life coming—that I would recognize it as a "crossroads" moment: you know, some kind of sign—a cloud that looked like a wise man, a piece of toast with a holy image burned into one side, a glimmer in a stranger's knowing eye—something. As it turns out, there was nothing that looked any different in my house on that morning as compared with any other day.

Instead, I engaged what was going on *inside my body*, as my logical head battled my intuitive gut. It was as if there were two completely different people in there with opposing points of view, debating to see who would win.

My head started louder with, "Take your train. It's a great intention but you don't need to do anything today. It's the thought that counts. No big deal. Take your normal train."

On any other day, it would have been easy to simply agree and have my wife take me to my train, letting another good intention slip by.

However, for some reason, that morning was different. Something inside my whole body stirred (another sign?) and stopped my internal chatter dead in its tracks. I looked at her and saw that nothing was more important than keeping my breakfast plans. "No," I said. "The whole point of the morning was to have breakfast together, so let's have breakfast together. I'll catch the next train as planned."

It was a simple declaration, a seemingly innocent decision.

For the next twenty minutes, we had a wonderful time together having breakfast in our small dining room. It was a beautiful morning, and I could not stop looking over at my family and just smiling. I was completely filled with love. My wife and I met on a ninth-grade trip to Quebec, and I knew that she was "the one" the first moment I saw her. Here we were, eighteen years later, and I was living the reality of my dreams. It was one of those moments of pure appreciation for what I had. I loved my life—not my job or my commute—but life was good! I remember thinking that it was amazing how such a small decision could shift my whole sense of being. In fact, this was the best I had felt in a long time.

After breakfast, my wife dropped me off at the station and I took the train into New York City, smiling the whole way. I'm sure I looked out of place among the cranky faces of the other commuters who were beaten down by the many hours they had spent getting in and out of the city at such a cost. But nothing could bother me that day—I had regained control of my life and I felt nothing but love inside. I felt great!

I made it into New York City, got on the subway, and, instead of being in my office, I was still underground when the first plane slammed into the North Tower of the World Trade Center, into my floor, *hitting my desk!* The morning I had chosen to have breakfast with my family was Tuesday, September 11, 2001. Yes—that is how fast it can happen. That is how unexpectedly it can come. We don't have endless tomorrows.

When I exited the subway, I stood across the street from the building, watching, as if it were a movie, not truly believing that on any other day, it would have been me up there. I couldn't imagine what it must have been like on the inside—that view I had known so well, up on the 96th floor.

Since that view will never be known again, I'm going to share a little bit of what it was like working from such a majestic viewpoint. On windy days, you could feel the building sway slightly and could often look outside of the window and see small planes and helicopters flying well below you. But there was never any fear. The sunsets from up there were some of the most magnificent I'd ever seen—the whole left half of the floor would turn orange and red as the sun beamed through uninterrupted—so much so that most times people would have to lower the shades in order to see their computer screens, many times annoyed and complaining about having to do so. Thinking back now, that seems absurd—shutting out nature's miracle in order to salvage fifteen more minutes of staring into a lifeless screen. But at the time, it seemed all too normal.

Now, that beautiful view is gone forever.

So there I stood, from a less familiar, outside-in perspective, looking up at my world that had a gaping hole where I should have been, not being able to comprehend what had happened and whom it had happened to. My perspective had shifted on September 10th when I had had a vision of having breakfast with my family. On September 11th, that perspective was solidified, never to reverse.*

Responsibility, Not Fate

When I share my story with others, whether it's a large audience at a conference or a single person, I am often told that I was meant to be saved, or that God has plans for me, or that I have an angel on my shoulder looking out for me, or something to that effect.

While I'd like to believe those statements, I can't accept them outright. The people I knew that worked with me were simply not as lucky that day. How can I have been meant to be saved while none of them were given that same offer? I knew them. I heard their life stories—saw their passion and commitment, shared pictures of our beautiful families with each other, spent 70% of my waking hours with them. I'm no more special than they were. They were me, they were you, they were us.

So rather than spending more time looking back and saying, "Why?" "Why did that happen?" "Why me?" and "Why them?" I have to accept that I am here. I am alive. I have a beautiful family, great friends, and

---

a meaningful mission. And I have a responsibility to look *forward* and say, "What now?" "What will I do with this opportunity—with this *gift* that I've been given?"

You have been given that same chance! Today is your gift!

Life is all about balance. Shouldn't you make sure your plans include a mix of joy, satisfaction, and service today? If you tilt too far in any direction, you are missing out on one or more aspects of your life. Tomorrow is not guaranteed. Plan for tomorrow but live today.

"FINE" Is a Four-Letter Word

Some of you who are reading this book may think your life is fine. That's okay. But I invite you to take a deeper look at why you've chosen to stop at *fine*.

I say *fine* is a four-letter word. We get lured into *fine's* lair, giving us just enough success, just enough happiness, and just enough comfort to get sleepy. It makes us complacent, tricking us into believing that *fine* is where we need to remain. It starts planting its roots into us, making us attached to the way things are in our fine life. It deprives us of the urgency we once felt to create more for our lives! It skews our vision and thoughts into believing that we must defend *fine* at all costs and that more than *fine* is dangerous, even selfish. We start to worry about what we're risking if we seek more, aim higher, and play bigger.

Things were fine for John. I met him at a talk I was giving and he challenged this concept, telling me that he was perfectly pleased; his life was fine. I asked him to discuss this further and he shared that he was in the mortgage business, working 10–12 hour days in a job that was paying the bills. He and his wife were okay—no major fights—his days and weeks ran pretty smoothly, and, basically, things were fine. As he shared the details of his life, he was leaning back in his chair, hands crossed behind his head, one ankle resting on the knee of his other leg.

Then I invited John to tell me about something he really loved that he hadn't done in a long time. At first, he had a hard time remembering. But as I continued to probe, the lost dreams started surfacing to the top. He shared that he had always loved coaching high school football and did it for years but gave it up when it became harder to earn a living in his industry. Money was tight and he had to focus all of his time on the job. Exploring his love of coaching further, he described how he could spend endless hours designing plays and game plans, being outside working with the kids, and keeping himself and the team fit, strong, and active. By now, he was sitting upright, legs uncrossed, hands moving around energetically. This was a different man in front of me. I yelled "STOP!" and had him become aware of how his energy and presence had shifted, something that was very obvious to everyone in the room except himself. John thought that *fine* was enough—but was it? His very energy as he began to talk about coaching—a long-lost passion—said differently.

When fear and need are leading the way—informing your decisions, your mood, your perspective, and the very nature of your purview—*fine* seems pretty good. *Fine* is safe; it is familiar. It feeds us, it provides shelter, and it gives us a place to catch our breath. There is a very useful place for *fine* within the context of our lives.

But what if we lose everything that has made our lives *fine*? What if we risk *fine* and lose? Can't you hear your parents (or friends or in-laws—insert your own influences here) telling you, "I told you so! You couldn't be happy with what you had? You had to have more? You're selfish. You're only thinking about yourself." On and on they go, with the limiting perspective that has kept them right where they are, the Mayors of Fineville.

I say that *fine* is not enough. Indeed, it has a very important role to play as we are rebounding from certain experiences. It is a wonderfully welcome plateau and safe haven in which to recharge, refocus, and begin to rebuild. But our vision and our aim need to be for more than fine. Otherwise, we risk the notion of looking back on the decades of *fine* and asking ourselves with the hard-earned wisdom of our years, "What the hell was I so afraid of?"

Ask any eighty or ninety-year-old and they'll tell you. I have yet to meet one of them that told me they would strive lower if they could do it all again. The recurring theme in those I've spoken with has been that they would be less afraid to try more things. They would not be beholden to their assumed limits and boundaries. They would have squeezed more life out of life. That is not *fine*.

As an example, look at school-aged kids. I have two wonderful children and, in hearing the daily drama of their lives, I think back as to how I would do it all again so differently. I would be more confident—real confidence, not merely a façade that I'd live into. I would take more chances, ask more girls out, and be more aggressive at the plate playing baseball.

So what's the difference between you looking at kids and an older person looking at you? You have this opportunity to be that person you would have been—now! *Fine* has a place, but it is a holding space, not a destination.

Today Is Your WakeUp Call!

Are you going to spend more time wishing your life was different in some way or hoping to make changes *one day*—after the kids get older, or once things at work settle down, or next month, or next year, or *some day*?

Unfortunately, I have some bad news for you. That day, *some day*, is never going to come. If you keep falling back on the attitude that you can accomplish what you really want someday, you're going to wake up five years from now and look back and wish you started five years earlier (and aren't you already doing that?) I say, look past those excuses. You have a chance to *rewrite your future* . . . now!

You don't need a tragedy *in* your life to wake up to the possibility that exists *for* your life. Did I see my wakeup call coming? Absolutely not! Was I living my life like I had *endless tomorrows*? Yes, I was! I got lucky. But I also got in action and I made that small decision to have breakfast with my family, which ultimately saved my life.

What is it time for you to put out into the world? What are you being a little hesitant about declaring because it would make it *too real* or it might actually put you on the hook for it? Look around. Really look. What are the signs you have been missing? What is it time for you to see?

Life is a gift and every single day counts. We think and we act like we have endless tomorrows, but we don't. We can't afford to waste our time or energy looking back and asking, "Why?" Instead, we need to look forward and say, "What now? Where do I want to go? What shall I do with this gift I've been given?"

September 10th was my wakeup call—a day that looked like any other day. Today is yours. What are you going to do with it?

2

Embrace the Storm

"In the middle of difficulty lies opportunity."
~Albert Einstein

To this day, I still look back and think about how important the events of 9/11 were in setting the course for my life. I'm not happy that 9/11 occurred. I don't wish that kind of experience on anyone. I don't wish for the loss, pain, and sadness felt by the families and friends of those lost or felt by the entire country at that time. I wish all of my colleagues were still alive.

But I know that none of that can occur. With my reluctant acceptance of that, I have been able to allow for the idea that 9/11 was one of the most important experiences I have ever had. It has made me who I have become. And, so, I uncomfortably embrace that storm, knowing that with the terrible loss and sadness it created it has also enabled tremendous growth and positive change for me.

Many times when clients come to me, it is because they are in the middle of a loss and they need some help making their way through. It is possible that you found your way to this book because you too are in the middle of a loss right now—or what I would call a "storm."

If you find yourself in that situation, this chapter can help you shift your perspective and view the storm differently, so you can learn and grow from it rather than simply escape it. If you are coming to this book from a steadier setting, this chapter can help you prepare for the inevitable storms that will come during the process of change as you navigate into the future.

A Look at the Storm Map

A storm is one of those times when it feels as though everything has come undone. It stirs up a swirl of emotion in us—anger, sadness, fear, mistrust, hopelessness, regret, confusion, disconnectedness, and more—all of which can be piled up into a big heap of overwhelm.

Examples of storms can include getting laid off from work, the betrayal of a trusted friend, having to declare bankruptcy, losing your house to foreclosure, the breakup of a once-loving relationship, or finding out someone you care about is gravely ill; the list can go on and on.

Understandably, we tend to keep our heads down during the storm, often shifting into survival mode. We can't even entertain the thought of taking on significant life changes since most of our energy is focused on the emotion of just trying to survive the storm. This is a time when *fine* becomes a place to catch your breath. In fact, initially, we may be fighting hard just to get back to a place where things are fine again.

What is it about these storms that are so scary and uncomfortable? Usually, it's because something is changing and it is outside of your control. During a storm, people experience things like:

- fear of the unknown
- fear of loss
- fear of the worst-case scenario or any bad outcome occurring
- lack of ability to control the change

- fear of disruption—a situation that ends up being worse than the current one
- concern over a change's impact on loved ones.

When a storm comes, there are real fears, there are real concerns, and there are real consequences.

Yet, as uncomfortable as the storm can be, there is almost always room for positive growth to come from it once it has passed through. As I reflect upon the storms that have shaped my own life, I notice that they have occurred to force me onto my true path.

Look for the Silver Lining

We all know someone who had a difficult experience but then, down the road, came to feel glad that it had occurred. If it hadn't happened, the person would never have <met the person of one's dreams, moved to that great town, traveled overseas, discovered that new career, or—fill in the blank here>.

During the last economic crisis, many people, including some of my friends and family, lost their jobs. They experienced a range of emotions at the time—some were devastated, some were terrified, and some were humiliated and embarrassed. The more they resisted and were victimized by what had happened *to them*, the more paralyzed and depressed they became.

For most, there was an initial period of shock and a wave of fear. When they looked around, nobody was hiring, more and more people were in the same situation, the media was painting a very dire picture of the outlook, and everything seemed to be moving in a negative direction.

Yet, some of my friends approached the situation a little differently. They made a conscious decision to let go of their fear and self-judgment and seized it as an opportunity to create something new. They embraced the storm.

I'm not saying they were irresponsible or reckless about their situations or how their financial snapshots affected their families. They networked, they tightened their budgets, and they did whatever they could to minimize the pain and loss. But they didn't stop there.

Dennis rediscovered his music. He began drumming in a band. This gave him a sense of purpose and renewed his spirit, and this positive flow of energy showed up in his job search and his interviews and he actually found more than one opportunity for himself.

Mark rediscovered that he loved to write and, after submitting a few articles to the local newspaper, he was awarded a monthly column. While that alone couldn't pay his bills, it brought him an enormous amount of satisfaction, rekindled his confidence, and helped him regain his sense of identity. Shortly thereafter, he got another job as a publisher with a very well-known magazine.

For me personally, during that financial storm, my key offerings at the time—coaching and speaking services—were some of the first things that businesses were cutting back on. I was not immune from the long tentacles of this global event, and I quickly went from having a comfortable twelve-month pipeline of business lined up to almost nothing in a matter of weeks.

At the time, these circumstances were pretty devastating. My wife and I realized that if we didn't do something quickly, we were at risk of losing our house. We both felt many fears during that time. Rather than accept the worst outcome as the only possible outcome, we got creative and found a way to keep our house and also explore places we've always dreamed of living. We turned a potential crisis into what turned out to be a very positive, life-changing experience.

I have seen many happy outcomes for people who have chosen to embrace the storm. New jobs, new relationships, a new spirit and self-awareness, or increased strength and resilience—the list goes on and on. What I have seen time and again is that the challenges we face today can turn into important life events, maybe even blessings, tomorrow.

Consider the following example of embracing the storm:

- The terror you may have felt upon getting laid off (from a job you didn't love) forces you to re-evaluate your career and you end up on a more meaningful path;
- The financial hardship and reduced spending ultimately get you to see how you've been living above your means and forces you to reprioritize what's really important to you;
- The foregoing of that vacation creates the possibility of spending some time at home, enjoying mealtime, playing games, and talking with your family and friends (very European of you), and you've never felt closer to your life partner or your children as you do now.

One of the worst storms imaginable is losing a loved one. In the following examples, there are two extreme stories of this experience and a description of how friends and family were somehow able to get past the anger and sadness by creating in their loved ones' honor something that now impacts so many others in a positive way.

First, you may have heard about what happened to Daniel Pearl, the *Wall Street Journal*-ist who was killed on TV by terrorists in 2005. Friends started a FODFest in their backyards (Friends of Danny Festival) as an informal backyard jam as a tribute in Danny's honor. The FODFest has grown into an internationally touring, non-profit organization with diverse programming initiatives that strengthen communities through music. It has literally touched thousands of people. Pearl's loss was tragic—clearly a storm in the worst sense of the word—and yet his friends were able to "embrace" that storm and bring some good out of it.

Second, there was Myles Beckley. Myles was only five years old when he was killed in a freak horseback riding accident on vacation with his family. Myles was a special little kid, touching the hearts of everyone he met with his warmth and his genuine smile. His father, Jay, has created a foundation in his son's honor to continue to spread the joy that Myles brought to others. The SMyles Scholarship Fund provides full-tuition scholarships and works to inspire youth in sports throughout Metro Detroit.

Just as the pain and loss of 9/11 was truly unbearable and the events of that day created a massive storm in many Americans' lives, those who loved Myles Beckley and Daniel Pearl had to contend with their own terrible storms after these individuals' unexpected loss. The point is that these folks didn't stop there. They didn't fold and disappear, throw in the towel, or give up on life. Instead, they resolved to create something positive. They started working their way through things by embracing the storm and seeing where they could create some good out of it.

Don't get me wrong. I know that loss is real. You will need time to experience it, grieve it, and work through it. Loss must be felt and expressed for it to be healed. I just don't want you to become a prisoner of it. You deserve much more than that.

So my hope for you is that you will allow yourself to experience the loss and also use that time as an opportunity to:

- acknowledge the love you have in your life
- relearn how to enjoy simple pleasures
- reach out to that friend you haven't spoken with in a while just to say you were thinking about him or her
- restart your exercise program
- re-center yourself around your true values.

This is your chance to be good to yourself and re-engage what is most important to you. You know deep down what is best for you—what brings you a sense of peace and health and wellness. Get in touch with what makes you feel good inside and give yourself those things as gifts to help you as you walk through the storm.

I have friends who believe that everything happens for a reason. I'm not sure I believe in the pre-destiny of all things, but I do believe that with each situation we stand in a new place, surrounded by choices and options that wouldn't have been possible unless all that had happened up to that point had actually occurred.

The very storm you are in the midst of may end up being a course correction for your life—one for which you may look back and feel forever grateful. Like my friends who lost their jobs in the economic crisis, or my wife and I during that same period, you can pay heed to the current situation—even worry about it, because that's just plain natural—but try, too, to avoid getting totally sucked into negativity so that it robs you of the vitality you need to redesign the life you want to move into.

I invite you to look at the storms you've faced and survived and see how they've shaped you. What events occurred as a result of any one of them that wouldn't have occurred otherwise? How did that experience actually *serve you*, even with all of the pain, loss, and hardship that may have come with it?

Embrace Your Own Storm

Let's see if we can cause a small shift in your perspective of a storm you've faced in the past (or are facing today). It's important to remember that by doing this, you are not saying that any loss, hardship, or pain that you or a loved one has experienced makes you happy. We're trying to take a different view of the experience to see what has risen in the space created by that storm.

For example, if it was the loss of a job, did that cause you to develop new skills, move to a new location, meet new people, or finally pursue that career that you've always wanted but never tried? If it was the loss of a loved one, what qualities of yours came forth that enabled you to deal with that situation? Strength? Resilience? Leadership? Compassion?

Reflect on the following questions:

- What part of you developed as a result of this experience?
- What motivation or clarity did this experience provide for you regarding changing the priorities in your life?
- What surprised you about yourself with regard to (1) how you handled the experience; (2) how you felt about the experience; and (3) what you did or didn't do as a result of the experience?

Conclusion

On your path to an extraordinary life, there are sure to be storms. But remember, with the storm comes learning and growth. Without having experienced many of the storms in my own life, I wouldn't now have the mental fortitude, strength, or vision to persist on this path that I'm on.

So the shift in perspective that I am inviting you toward—one in which you embrace rather than run from the storm—is that the storm can be the very catalyst that springboards you into the next phase of your extraordinary life.

While you may not have the ability to truly embrace the storm as you are enduring it, understand that there is something powerful waiting for you on the other side. When the rain finally stops and the blue skies start peeking through again, you can begin seeking those gifts awaiting your discovery and you can begin to bring them to life. Your life.

3

You Have the Power

"I am the master of my fate; I am the captain of my soul."
~"Invictus" by William Ernest Henley

How would you feel if I told you that you have everything you could possibly need *right now* to create your extraordinary life? Would you feel excited? Would you feel relieved? Would you be skeptical or doubtful? The truth is that some of what you need is all around you waiting to be discovered or employed; but much of what you need is already inside of you. *You* have the power to create your extraordinary life.

I'd like to give you an example of what I mean. We start on one late Autumn morning when I lived in New York City. As I walked to the subway from my apartment, I noticed that no one around me was smiling. In fact, everyone had either an angry, bothered, or apathetic look on their faces. I have grown up in and around New York City and it always strikes a nerve when non-New Yorkers tell me how nasty everyone is and what a cold and hard city it is. I always defend the people and the city because I know it isn't true—you just have to break through the surface. But for some reason, that day, the lack of warmth I felt from my fellow Upper West Siders made me angry. I thought, "Maybe my friends are right—this *is* a cold, hard place!" and that upset me.

I didn't want to live in a neighborhood like that. I wanted to be in a place where people cared about each other and where people smiled and said hello to each other—even as strangers. As I continued my trek to the train, I was getting more and more upset as I traveled each block with the same dissatisfying result. Maybe I was naïve in wanting New York City to be more like Small Town, USA, where everyone actually does smile and say hello to each other, but that day—as not a single person smiled at me, let alone said hi—I was getting furious!

And then I passed my reflection in the side of a building. What I saw there absolutely amazed me! Looking back at me was a bitter, angry, and tired man. Who was that miserable guy? In that moment, I realized that I had a bigger scowl on my face than anyone I had just passed! No wonder no one was smiling at me—I looked angrier and more bothered than they did.

It was like having cold water splashed in my face. (Thanks, I needed that!) So at that very moment I decided to conduct a very simple experiment. I decided that for the rest of my commute to work that day, I was going to smile and say "good morning" to as many people who passed by me as possible. I wouldn't worry about whether they were looking at me or what kind of expression they were wearing or anything else. I would just look right into their eyes and say "good morning" and "hello" without any expectations of a response.

For the next fifteen minutes, I did just that. I smiled and said "good morning" or "hello" to almost everyone I passed. What happened was *amazing*!

A few of the people looked at me with this puzzled look on their faces. For some, their immediate, uncontrolled reaction was to put their hand on their pockets to protect their wallets. Some looked behind them as if I were speaking to someone else. Some turned away, some grunted, and one even crossed the street to avoid me, muttering under his breath as he scampered away. But, for about half of the people to whom I had offered this greeting, no matter what expression they had on their faces prior, it just melted away, and a big, warm smile replaced it. Many of them even said hello back to me.

Through a few simple gestures, I had created the very neighborhood I was seeking. Most importantly, I learned that I had the power to create that neighborhood any time I desired. That morning was an incredible lesson in my own potential to influence the world in which I live.

But let me tell you something. You have the same "magical" power to influence the world around you as I did. The energy you put out there, the way you talk to and look at other people, and the change you generate through your own actions all affect your environment.

The power to create an extraordinary life is within your reach! It's in *your* control.

In this chapter, my goal is to help you understand this amazing power you have to create the life you crave. We will explore the rich abundance of what you already have in your possession and the strengths and accomplishments that you can already call your own so that you can start this journey from a place of joy and confidence.

Then, we will roll up our sleeves together, take out the detective tools, and look inward at how you are currently contributing—or not contributing—to the extraordinary life you seek. The rest of this chapter provides a number of practical tools that can help you shift your mindset and your behavior toward creating the environment (or neighborhood) you are seeking.

You see, it's really all about you. That's not to say that you don't have to deal with external events or even other people who may not have the best intentions for you. That's not to say that life won't throw you some curveballs—and we already know there will be plenty of storms. What I'm trying to say is, if you want to live out the life of your biggest, boldest dreams, then you gotta steer the ship.

Here we go . . .

Grab an Oar

A lot of times, we are unconsciously being observers and commentators in our lives, just watching as the ticker tape of life goes across our screen. Many of us put our own sense of vitality, joy, and ease into the control of other people, things, events, and measurements. We blame it on the boss, the life partner, the stage of life, the lack of money—whatever—and then act as if we have no ability to change or influence it. In other words, we make ourselves the victim. In blaming others, though, we give up our personal power to someone else. Why would we do that?

Don't you want to be the one in charge of your own life and its outcomes? Of course you do. Inherent in being responsible for your life is the reality that you *must steer*. You cannot just float down the river. You need to grab the oars! That requires vision. It also requires *accountability*—the focus of the present chapter—and a good measure of courage.

As Gandhi once said, "Be the change you wish to see in the world." That means that each one of us is responsible for making this world, and our lives, what we want them to be. As the story that opened this chapter demonstrated, we cannot just sit there and wish something would change or hope something will change. We have to create that change! Instead of just wishing I lived in a neighborhood where everyone smiled and said "good morning," I decided to *create* it. I chose to be accountable for making it exist. I stopped merely *reacting* to everything and started *creating*.

What I want for you to see is that your life as you know it—for better and for worse—is your own. There are moving parts and other people—challenges and obstacles—you will need to deal with, but you have to take the helm if you really do want to create that extraordinary life you've been seeking. This means appreciating what you have *and* recognizing your ability to bring new and different things into your life. If you are not yet where you want to be in your life, you've got to get rowing. Load up the boat with all the good stuff you already have; accept, influence, or toss the other stuff (more on that technique later in the chapter), and then start moving.

It may be a little intimidating at first. In fact, you may get a little stressed or anxious thinking about doing something that's out of your comfort zone. But I have to tell you, the more you do it, the easier it becomes. In my neighborhood example above, by the third city block, saying hello was almost effortless. I just needed to get over that initial hump. I was so much closer than I had thought!

This new responsibility—what we call *accountability* in the coaching world—is yours for the taking. We often equate "accountability" with blame and blamelessness. By assuming that everyone should say hello to me, in the previous example, I blamed them for how they were being. In that moment, I gave away my power. By blaming them, I was saying that I had no ability to change the situation.

When I took a different tact, by taking responsibility for how I was being, I took back the power and essentially declared, "I am responsible for everything that happens in my life." By making that shift, and smiling at everyone first, I actually *caused* the reactions others were having to me. The reactions were varied and unpredictable, but had I done nothing, I would have created nothing. Instead, I transformed my intention into a reality that many people were happy and friendly in New York City, and I was one of them. As a result of my action, I left a trail of warm expressions in my wake.

The fun part is thinking that the experience the passersby had with me spilled over into the rest of their day. Because they started the day with a smile, it probably rippled throughout the rest of their day and influenced everyone they touched and everything they did all day long! That simple act of smiling first and inviting others to join in may have touched thousands of people that morning! Who knows? Why not?

The Power of Acknowledgment: Stop Focusing on the Gaps

Part of taking back the power is learning how to see the rich abundance that already exists in your life. What are you good at? Great at? What things are going well? Where are your strengths and how are you employing them? What potential is waiting to be opened up and explored?

Many times, when my clients are stuck, there's a common theme going on where they are constantly focusing on all things as being half-empty. They feel less successful than their peers; they look at their neighbor's house with envy; they focus on everything they haven't done or achieved. There's always another prize waiting around the corner if they could just move a little faster. There's always more they could be doing, more they could have accomplished, more they could be, if only . . .

Sound familiar?

It is easy to look around and see only the problem, the shortcoming, or the gap. But once you place your focus there, you become blind to the substance and good that is there as well. You can get stuck focusing on what's missing or what didn't go right—and end up either beating yourself up, blaming someone or something for your situation, or worse—creating a sense of hopelessness and powerlessness. Do this enough and you'll start anticipating negative outcomes, bad experiences, and poor results, trapping you into this mindset and creating a vicious cycle.

Yes, there is a benefit to this kind of attitude and thinking—you get to avoid accountability and get to blame everyone and everything for your situation. You get to make everyone wrong. You get to be the victim.

However, there is also a significant cost to this type of thinking. When you bring this "focusing on the gap" attitude to your life, you dis-empower yourself. You fall prey to your own perspective, measuring your worth by what you don't have, haven't done, and haven't yet climbed. Doesn't it make a lot more sense to measure your life by what is already in it?

To see what I mean, let's imagine you are climbing a mountain with other people. In fact, every person in the world is on this mountain. As you look up, you see all of those people that have climbed higher than you and you think, "if only I was as high as they are," "if only I was as good as they are," "if only I had what they had." But—and this is important—as you reverse your gaze and look down the mountain to those below, you will hear the *exact same thing being said about you*: "If only I was where that person is . . ."

Dr. Art Brownstein, MD, a pioneer in self-healing, believes that, "When we focus on what we don't have, we create scarcity in our lives and will always feel insecure with our situation. By seeing that your life is full today, you will understand that abundance is not measured by your resources but through your ideas about your life."[1]

Too many times we focus on what we don't have versus what we do have. Kicking yourself for everything you didn't do and what you have *yet* to accomplish is not the way to get there. I want you to focus, instead, on what you already bring to the journey. This is going to get you revved up for the ride, full of the energy you'll need to make this trek, rather than make you feel less-than or depleted.

By continuing to appreciate the positive things in our lives by staying present and using consistent effort, we will see our lives change, and even completely transform, bringing us more freedom and a lot more control. We can be thankful, we can give ourselves some much needed credit, and we can even be excited that we have something to enjoy. We can stop and appreciate what we have instead of dwelling on what's missing or wrong.

I want to encourage you to create this powerful mind-shift toward focusing on—not the gaps or negative space—but the rich topography that is currently your life. What is filling all of that positive space? Small or large, start to think about where your strengths, gifts, blessings, and accomplishments lie. Family? Friends? Home? Job? Neighborhood? Only you can know where the abundance lies, but I guarantee you if you stop long enough to look, you will find it. You simply need to start viewing the world differently.

STOP! READ THIS.

My clients--even my high-powered business-owner clients and corporate stars--tell me often that one of the most powerful exercises I introduce them to is to engage in a practice of daily acknowledgement. They tell me that this exercise stops them from constantly beating themselves up and helps restore their confidence, especially when things aren't "perfect" or done to their high (and often unrealistic) expectations.

So stop reading and take a moment to respond to this question: *What do you want to acknowledge yourself for?*

It can be what you did (or didn't do), how you acted or reacted, who you were being, anything. Think...write... meditate. It doesn't matter how you express yourself, as long as you do something. This is the one chance you get to stop rushing through your day. Take advantage of it.

Remember, this is *safe space*—your own little sanctuary for you to experiment and explore in. You don't have to share anything you write with anyone if you don't want to, and you don't have to be perfect here. But isn't it time to be authentic—especially with yourself? Don't worry, I'll wait.

Don't "Should" on Others

In addition to focusing on the gaps, another mindset that tends to keep us stuck is when we point blame outward to those around us—I call this "shoulding" on others.

Have you ever heard yourself saying,

> "He should do that."
> "She should act that way."
> "If only he did that differently, my life or job would be better."
> "It's her fault that I'm not happy."

This is "shoulding" on others. When you "should" on others, you are putting the locus of control outside of yourself, which is shorthand for saying that . . . you are blaming everybody else! That is not fair to the people around you. Plus, it's counterproductive. As long as you are out there in the world "shoulding" on others (that's not a pretty sight, is it?), you are robbing yourself of your power to affect a situation and create the life you want for yourself.

Let me tell you a story that reveals just how mixed up we all can get when we start to "should" on others.

Back in the mid-1990's, when the Internet was brand new to most businesses, I worked at a big company and was in charge of creating my division's website. I enjoyed a lot of latitude in managing this big project. One day, I got a new boss who had a great reputation and I was told how lucky I was to be getting her as my manager. She seemed nice, but right away she wanted me to check in with her on everything I was doing. Every decision I made had to be run by her now. I felt completely stifled, mistrusted, and unmotivated in my new situation. The joy I had had in the job disappeared and I started to lose interest in my work. I felt that I *should* be allowed to maintain my autonomy, I *should* still be the one to make the decisions, my boss *should* manage me differently, and it was because of her that I had become unhappy in my role.

I saw this as the truth. My boss was the cause, and I was the victim. When a position became available in another division, I jumped at the chance to switch roles and go to another department. I spent the next six months avoiding my now former boss and feeling partially angry, partially ashamed. She didn't know what had happened to set me off, and I didn't explain it. But it was killing me to have this bad feeling inside me every time I saw her or passed my old floor.

One day, I took a deep breath and summoned the courage to walk into her office. I was nervous. I told her my story of what had happened and shared exactly how I felt and why I transferred to another department. She smiled, came over to me, and told me that the reason she had asked me to run everything by her was so she could learn about what I did. She wasn't intending to limit me at all. The Internet was new to her, and she thought I could teach her a lot by sharing my work and strategies. Wow. I was flabbergasted. What a misunderstanding!

That experience was difficult, yet it taught me how off-track we can get when we focus our energy on blaming others. What if I had taken accountability for how I had felt and spoken to her directly about it? By "shoulding" on my boss—"she *should* manage me differently," "she *should* know that I am proficient at my job," "she *should* give me more freedom"—I lost sight of my own ability to influence the situation.

Why is this shift in perspective so important? Because it gives you back your power and the freedom to choose how to act or react in any given situation. It allows you to take the control back and become the owner of your life, not the observer. As we mentioned earlier, we call this sense of agency and ownership *accountability*.

Accountability requires a powerful shift in perspective in how we view the world and circumstances as they occur. It's shifting from an outward-focused mentality where the proverbial finger is pointed out there—at someone or something and away from you—to the more empowering notion of inward-focused accountability . . . that you cause your life. The buck stops here (finger pointed toward you)!

Where are you effectively saying, "I am a victim," by blaming other people or conditions? Try shifting your perspective and point the finger back at yourself: What can you change or influence? How are you causing the situation? What can you do about it? By doing this, you are once again empowered to make a difference in your life regardless of the circumstances.

The Excuse Machine

Closely linked to our tendency to "should" on others is the ease with which we make up excuses for why we can't do certain things—I call this using our own personal "excuse machine." When the excuse machine kicks in, it stops us from taking action in our lives. We say things such as "I'm too old" or "I can't make a living doing that" or "I don't have time" to cover up a fear we may have and to justify our inactions.

Excuses are not the truth, however; they are faulty beliefs that we make up in our heads. Let me tell you a story to show how false the "I'm too old" excuse is, for example. Claude Choules published a book about his life entitled, *The Last of the Last*. What's interesting about that isn't the fact that he recalls times learning to surf in South Africa, buying cigarettes for a penny a pack, or seeing the first car ever driven through his Australian village. What's impressive is that he published this book when he was 108 years old. That's right, 108! Claude Choules died in 2011 as the last World War I veteran on record.

Many times as I'm helping my clients explore new possibilities for their careers and/or their lives, I am often hit with the "I'm too old for that" excuse, which feels very real to them. People are working longer into their sixties and beyond; even those of you in your forties and fifties may have decades of active work life in front of you (for better or worse). If you can broaden your perspective beyond what's immediately in front of you, you may find that developing new skills, going back to school part time, or getting certified in something new is not only possible but also a great way to disrupt your time running in place on the hamster wheel. When you view a twenty-year horizon, a two-year training program still leaves plenty of time to reap the benefits of that investment of time, money, and energy.

When you're feeling like you're too old to change, remember:

- You're not starting over; you're leveraging all you've done to repurpose skills for your new path.
- Your excuse machine may try to tell you why change is dangerous or irresponsible. But what's the real cost? Waking up five years from now, saying, "What was I waiting for? What was I so afraid of?"
- Two words: *Claude Choules*. If our 108-year-old friend could write and publish a book at his age, think of what you can do.

What's stopping you from taking action in your life? What logic are you using to justify your actions or your complacency?

I've discovered that my number one excuse has been "I'm not interested." That was the one I pulled off the shelf more than any other. Oh yeah, I was really good at "not being interested" in things. For example, early on when someone suggested I take my message out to the corporate arena in the form of public speaking, I said, "I'm not interested in that." It was only when my mentor challenged me to look inward that I realized that I actually *was* interested, *but afraid* of failing or looking foolish. The excuse "I'm not interested" actually *protected* me from making myself look bad. It gave me an out for not even trying. It kept me safe and warm and protected. Yet, as *A Message to Garcia* author Elbert Hubbard said, "The greatest mistake you can make in your life is to continually fear you will make one."

What I didn't realize at the time was that this excuse had a cost. It kept me disengaged and complacent. I never would have experienced public speaking as a new outlet for my message or a new revenue stream for my business had I not become aware of my excuse machine.

I discovered that as important as it was to understand how using that excuse was protecting and benefiting me, I needed to become aware of the costs too. Yes, I was spared from the possibility of failing or feeling humiliated, but at the cost of not learning and experiencing new things, as well as missing out on the growth opportunity and confidence boost I would get from overcoming my fear and facing this particular challenge. As one of my mentors frequently reminds me, "experience creates confidence." Not the other way around.

Let's look at how these excuses give you the reason you need to avoid making a change or to keep making the same mistakes over again. This is an important exercise because becoming aware of your excuses and why you use them is the first step in taking your power back and can provide a huge breakthrough for you!

What Does Your *Excuse Machine* Look Like?

We all have our own version of the excuse machine. Mine has traditionally been, "I'm not interested." Using the table below, walk yourself through an excuse you often use. Then, reflect on what benefits you get by using this excuse. Lastly, capture the costs of this excuse by answering what your excuses keep you from doing/accomplishing/gaining. I've gotten you started by completing it for my own excuse.

EXCUSE:	BENEFITS: Using this excuse allows me to…	COSTS: Using this excuse keeps me from…
Example: "I'm not interested"	…not fail. If I don't try, I can't fail. It protects me from making myself look bad.	… learning and experiencing new things, as well as missing out on the growth opportunity and confidence boost I would get from overcoming my fear and facing a particular challenge.

Now that you've discovered your excuse machine, you have the power to challenge it. By recognizing the excuses you start to throw at yourself each time you have an inclination to do something new or different, and by understanding both the benefits as well as the costs of letting these excuses run the show, you gain the ability to make powerful new choices to clear away your self-imposed road blocks.

Change, Influence, or Accept

Once you stop pointing the blame outward toward others and you unplug your excuse machine, you free up your own potential to proactively create the life you want for yourself. You regain a sense of *agency* and *ownership*. You become clear that this is your life and you have the power to make things happen.

The key here is moving from being a *reactor* to being a *catalyst*—the one who causes actions and doesn't merely react to things. This allows you to shift from being a victim to being a student and adventurer in your own life.

One of the biggest complaints I hear from both my business and personal clients is that they are stuck in reactive mode, unable to get through the never-ending, incoming pile. They feel like they can't think proactively, and their creativity, innovation, and strategic mindset suffer because of it.

Yet, staying stuck in reactive mode is merely a symptom. As you stay in this mode—day after day, frenzied and frustrated, your tolerance temperature rises slowly over time, inching its way slowly to the dreaded melting point. Okay, that's a little dramatic, but if you really think about the impact this pace is having on you, just considering the health costs alone is pretty frightening. When we're talking about something as important as your health and well-being, that is definitely a situation where you do not want to wait for a near miss to get you to wake up and take this stuff seriously.

Think about it. What happens when a reactor overheats? There's a blowout, an explosion, a meltdown. How many times have you seen it in your coworkers, your spouse, or even yourself? This is when energy from one of your worlds spills over to the other worlds much like a radiation cloud and makes everything it touches toxic. You yell at the kids because you had a hard day at work. Your mind wanders, and you disengage from a meeting and then get defensive when called upon. You feel isolated, where nobody understands you. It's exhausting, it zaps the vitality out of you, and there's no sense of ease. Basically, it sucks.

I'm not committed to being an overheated reactor, and I know you're not either. So, here is a mind-shift that can help you make the move from reactor to catalyst: *For any given situation, you have three choices of how to interact with it. You can either change it, influence it, or accept it.*

That's it. Those three and those three alone. Let's explore . . .

Change It

In order to change something outright, you need to have the commitment, ability, and authority to implement change. For example, I decided I was going to take a different train the morning of September 11, 2001. I didn't have any meetings that I needed to attend so I simply changed the time I was going to leave for work on that day. Notice that I still had a mental tug-of-war that I needed to win, but I was wrestling against myself. My decision was completely within my control.

Where do you have the opportunity to change things directly rather than feel stuck or powerless? Are you making assumptions that limit your ability to create and implement some kind of change to your situation? We'll talk about the fears that hold us back later in the book, but I encourage you to push yourself and reconsider where you can actually make outright changes for yourself, even small ones.

Influence It

If you really are not able to change something outright, how can you begin to influence it? Your ability to influence something can happen in an instant, but, typically, it's more of a process. So don't get impatient and stuck because your first attempt to influence doesn't create immediate change.

In fact, the most effective way to influence something is to start by changing yourself (something very much within your ability to control). For example, I knew I couldn't just outright change my Upper West Side neighborhood to make it different. I couldn't control what other people did and said to me. I couldn't change their mood or temperament directly. They owned that. But I did realize that I could *influence* it, and by controlling my own actions and saying hello to passersby, I did succeed at influencing many of their moods and reactions all by changing myself (which, in turn, changed the neighborhood for that brief time).

Notice that I didn't get frustrated when people didn't return the gesture. I understood what I could control and what I couldn't. I let go of any expectations regarding how other people would respond to me. That gave me the freedom to continue to focus on the one thing I could control—my own actions—and not worry or react to those things I couldn't control—others' responses. It was definitely challenging at first, but I kept on going and saying hello, knowing that I had to let the process work and not base success or failure on any one moment in time, especially in the beginning with those first few hello's. Ultimately, through my own influence, I had created the change I sought.

Accept It

The third aspect is to accept things exactly as they are. This doesn't mean "tolerate" things, because if you are tolerating them, then you haven't really accepted them. In that case, you may want to summon the courage to try to influence them. What I mean by accept is to really take a look at yourself and see what is bothering you (or missing for you) regarding the situation, and see whether you are able to come to terms with it, as is. This happens all of the time in relationships.

Let's take a real example, a partner who snores (!), and use it for our purposes here.

First, you complain about the situation. ("I hate his snoring! It's loud and keeps me up. It sounds like there's a train coming through our bedroom!") The more you resist it, the worse it is for you and the more it upsets you.

Then, after your complaints don't make a dent in the situation, you try to change your partner's annoying habit outright. (That's when you kick him, turn him over, or pinch his nose.) Those tactics may succeed for a while, but you're still awake and it usually results in some resentment by your partner. Inevitably, it doesn't last as he goes back to his old ways. ("You're snoring again." "I can't help it!")

Next, you try to influence the situation by looking at what you can actually control. ("I'm going to wear ear plugs so I don't hear you snore anymore.") That has a better chance of succeeding because you are changing yourself and not trying to "fix" him, which by now you realize you can't do. That helps a lot, even if you sacrifice a little bit of ear comfort.

But every once and a while, you still have those times where even the thickest ear plugs can't keep out his buzz-sawing. But you love him and realize that he really can't help it, so you accept it. Rather than defining that as "giving up," it really means you've stopped trying to make him who you want him to be and have accepted the fact that he is the way he is. Once you fully accept his snoring (It exists! *C'est la vie!*), you stop fighting it mentally and your sleep improves.

Another example is at work. One of my clients, Tim, was frustrated because his boss kept skimming over all of the beautiful presentation slides he had put together and went directly to the financial pages. Tim felt that he wasted a lot of time putting those informational and visual slides together for her. When she bypassed all of them, he chose to make it mean that his ideas weren't being valued (notice the language I am using here—he was choosing to be a victim in this interaction with his boss).

However, as Tim and I further explored this situation, he realized that his boss was primarily accountable for specific financial hurdles and couldn't even consider ideas unless they met certain revenue goals. Once Tim understood this and accepted it, it allowed him to stop making his boss wrong and he shifted the way he presented her with information by moving the financial pages to the front of the presentation and putting the visual slides in the appendix for reference (i.e., Tim accepted and then accommodated the situation.) She responded very positively and they continue to have a much stronger working partnership than before.

The next time you find yourself getting stressed or unhappy in a situation—like the reactor that is ready to explode—take yourself through the following short exercise. Ask yourself, "Can I change it?" If the answer is yes, consider the options and take action. If not, ask yourself if you can influence things. Again, if yes, consider the options. If not, ask yourself whether this is something you are willing to accept. You can reclaim some of your peace of mind by accepting what you cannot change or influence and moving on from there. These three choices for interacting with the world—change, influence, and accept—will give you back your sense of control and power.

Conclusion

Sometimes we stop ourselves from trying something because we are afraid we won't be perfect. Sometimes we don't even attempt certain things because we're afraid of failing or looking foolish. We blame others, we play the role of victim, we pretend we're not interested, or we wait for the someday that may never come.

While it's useful to define the benefits of that kind of inhibited, fearful behavior, the costs are just too high. We're giving up all of our personal power when we hold ourselves back, when, in fact, personal power is the very thing we need to lead the way.

Make this the year you take your power back. It was there all the time! Just like Dorothy in *the Wizard of Oz*, she always had the power to go back home in her ruby slippers . . . she just wasn't aware of it.

Living an extraordinary life means being accountable for *creating* an extraordinary life. Take hold of the wheel and steer your ship! After all, you have nothing to lose but that same pattern from which you're trying to break free.

4

The Art of Disruption

"You can never cross the ocean unless you have the courage to lose sight of the shore."

~Christopher Columbus

When I was a boy, my dad always told me, "Never set a pattern." While he did this to give himself an excuse as to why he would often mistakenly pull into our neighbor's driveway instead of our own, my dad was unknowingly teaching me the concept of disruption: never set a pattern—in other words, take a different route.

In coaching terms, disruption means letting go of the comfortable patterns that are not serving us the way we need: having the same tired conversations with the same people, clinging to the same weekly routines, and going to the same life-sapping job day after day. We spend a lot of effort and time holding onto these patterns because as people, most of us crave the stability and familiarity of these structures. It taps into our ancient limbic brain and gives us a sense of safety and security.

Our ancestors may have experienced it like this: "Me see dinosaur, me run. Me see dinosaur again, me run . . ." This approach kept us from becoming lunch. What if we disrupted *that* pattern? "Me see dinosaur, me going to say hi." Not such a good idea. Disruption of the pattern plays into our deepest fears of survival because it means rocking a system that is proven to work. However, those innate behaviors that were once very useful may eventually become something of a handicap.

Once again, you are faced with the notion that everything has a benefit, but a cost as well. Think about some of the routines you are doing day to day, week to week. What benefits are you getting from them? What might be the cost? In other words, what are you missing by doing these things the same way over and over each time?

Disruption means being willing to let go of what you already know and the things you already do—maybe even cling to—in order to open up the space for something new and desirable to grow. In fact, when you start disrupting those patterns, you start to see new things ("I once was blind, but now I see").

In the earlier chapters, we discussed a mental shift in perspective. In this chapter, we're going to take a look at both the mental and physical acts of blowing up our comfortably rooted patterns and routines. We'll also explore the concept of letting go in order to bring a new understanding to those things that are blocking our progress so we can see that while they are actually trying to help us, the cost of keeping them around is just too high.

The Art Explored

One of the most powerful tools at your disposal when creating an extraordinary life is the ability to disrupt the familiar patterns of your day-to-day.

You know how when you take the same driving route many times, pretty soon you shift into automatic pilot and you stop seeing the things around you? Everything becomes a blur as you mentally drift. You may wonder how you got where you are since you don't even remember the ride. When you take a new way home, you become more alert and more present, and therefore notice things again. "Look how nice the view is from here" . . ."I always wondered where this road led" . . ."I never knew there was a restaurant there." So much lies undiscovered right in front of us.

An easy way to understand the benefits of disruption is by looking at how it applies to fitness. When exercising, there comes a point when your muscles stop growing and your fitness levels off and no longer improves. You keep working hard, doing your exercises, and trying to make health gains, but no matter how hard you try, you are stuck running in place at your current fitness level. Personal trainers call this "hitting a plateau." According to Brian Clapp, a fitness expert based in the beautiful Berkshire Mountains of Western Massachusetts, the trick is to continuously confuse your muscles in order to keep your gains steady and to avoid hitting that plateau. This serves to disrupt your body's efficiency with your current workout routine.

It's not that you're not working hard enough; it's that doing the same thing over and over stops producing results. Look at where you may be experiencing that in your life. How about in your work? It might be time to change up the routine. See, it's not about putting in more hours, it's about working and/or living differently than you have been. It's about blowing up your current routines and behaviors in order to clear room for something new: a fresh perspective, a new habit, and a new ritual. That is what leads to growth when you are stagnating and that is the principle of disruption.

In Chapter 2, I shared my experience of the storm I found myself in as a result of the economic crisis. As more and more of the conferences where I was scheduled to speak got canceled, I continued trying to generate new opportunities. Every day, faced with the specter of financial hardship, I was hitting the phones, working harder and harder to try to create something, to no avail. It came to the point where my wife and I finally realized that no matter how hard I was working, the opportunities just weren't there. It was time to make a change.

That was when we decided to completely disrupt our lives. We were living in a very beautiful part of Connecticut. It had everything you could dream of—a residents-only beach on the Long Island Sound with its own private island, sailing school, kayak rentals, and a golf course for residents. It had a beautiful river coursing through the middle of town, a thriving Main Street, outdoor concerts all summer, some of the best schools in the State, and on and on. It really is a premiere town.

So when we decided to leave, it was a very difficult decision. But we knew we had to disrupt our situation in order to be able to take control back of our lives. Using our knowledge of how to embrace a storm, we chose to see it as an opportunity instead of focusing on the loss it was creating. We also wanted to be sensitive to how these changes would affect our two kids, nine and six years old at the time. Knowing that we'd have to change our living situation, we redefined things as the opportunity to go on a Life Adventure as a family. And that is exactly what we did. Let the disruption begin . . .

We rented out our home and set out on our adventure. We had little stability but that also meant we had total freedom. In fact, when we were looking for the next place to move, we considered a variety of interesting places, such as Napa, Austin, the mountains and the beaches of North Carolina, Italy, Colorado . . . anything that we felt would be aligned with our core values (more on defining your core values in the next section of the book). So there we were, untethered and able to explore many possibilities.

Part of what my wife and I both feel strongly about is that a big component of our parenting responsibility is not only to keep our children safe (of course) but also to prepare them for what life throws at them. That means giving them plenty of opportunities to get out of their comfort zones and adapt to new situations. With this move, they were going to have to endure a storm . . . new home, new town, new school, new friends, and a new routine. We made sure that they not only felt supported, but that they got as much value from the experience as possible. We taught them, by example, that disruption makes you stronger—that when you get out of your normal routine, you grow.

So as I reflect upon the incredible growth my whole family has enjoyed in the past few years, I can attribute so much of it to our willingness to make those hard decisions and disrupt our comfortable life situation when it no longer served us. As a result, my children get to jump on the yellow bus every Tuesday after school and head to a nearby mountain for ski club. They are learning to define wealth as more than the number of zero's behind the family's bank account, to notice and appreciate when people are kind to them, to enjoy living in a natural setting that is majestic, and to know that dad will be there for most of their soccer/baseball games and school plays.

Being willing to disrupt the way things are—even though they feel safe, familiar, and comfortable—is one way to bring all that abundance and happiness into your life. Sometimes you have to get out of your life to really see your life. That's why it's important to take vacations, have down time, and slow down in order to look at the big picture.

To fully understand the concept of disruption, it helps to look at the *opposite* of disruption. The opposite of disruption can be described as:

- fear of change: doing what feels comfortable in order to avoid change
- fear of the unknown: clinging to what we know, not because we love it, but because we don't know what it will take, or what we might lose in order to change it
- inertia: doing things the way we always do them, because that's the way we always do them

- limiting beliefs and judgment: believing that things have to be a certain way, without exploring other possibilities
- overwhelm and paralysis: not knowing how to begin and using that as an excuse to not do anything about it.

The opposite of disruption is being stuck.

For those old enough, think back to when a record used to skip. If you never had the pleasure of listening to records, think of when a CD skips. Instead of the music continuing on as it should, the same lyrical phrase or little snippet of melody plays over and over again. It's maddening! Now think about what you can do when the record or CD starts to skip.

You have a few options. First, you can turn the volume lower (which many of us do when our lives are stuck in the same groove—we deny it, ignore it, don't deal with it, and say things are "fine"). Second, we can turn the music off, get completely numb to our reality, and check out, just going through the motions. Or, third, we can move the needle on the record player (or hit the fast-forward button on the CD player). However, in order to move the needle, we need to get up from where we're sitting, physically take the needle in our hands and then carefully lift and replace it down as close to the next groove as possible. We need to make a choice and take an action.

When you think about moving the needle, so to speak, what are some of your thoughts? "Don't scratch the record," "Don't break the needle," "Is this going to skip the next time I play this," "My favorite CD is ruined," etc. Guess what—this is a perfect example of disruption. It takes intention and physical effort to "move the needle," and, in the process, many fears will surface. However, the benefits are clear: you get to listen to a new song; you become energized by a new beat; and you feel like life is moving forward, not standing still.

Now let's take the record analogy further—you don't always have to wait for the record to skip to disrupt the groove. What if you don't like the next song? Life is the same way. You don't have to wait to get fired, become sick, or have some other grand wakeup call to choose to move the needle—or even change the record! Disruption is about being willing to shift out of the inertia of today's routine and generate momentum toward something different and new, purely because you want to!

What Can You Disrupt?

Write down three habits, routines, or behaviors where disruption would benefit you:

1.

2.

3.

For each one, identify the key force that's kept you stuck there. Was it a fear? Inertia? Overwhelm? A belief or truth of what would happen if you did something different?

What may be the benefits of disrupting each one? What makes that important for you?

Holding on to Letting Go

At its core, the art of disruption involves letting go: letting go of fear, letting go of judgment, and letting go of control over the outcome. It involves letting go of all the blocks that are stopping you from making the changes needed in order to create the life you really want. Sounds easy right? It's not.

The first step is to develop an awareness of your fears and blocks and recognize them for what they are . . . fears and blocks. Nothing more. The next step is to begin to let go and see that on the other side is something good, rewarding, and exciting.

Just as I encouraged you in Chapter 2 to *embrace the storm*—to recognize that challenging times bring growth and to be willing to go through those challenging times rather than escape them by the shortest route—I also want you to consider the possibility of *letting go* of those blocks that are holding you back.

What is preventing you from making a change? Here's a list of some of the common things that stop people:

- "What if I fail? My family is counting on me."
- "What if I hate the new job more than the one I already have?"
- "My boss will never let me try something new."
- "I'm not smart or creative enough."
- "I'm too old. I already missed that window."
- <add yours here . . . >

Some of these blocks are related to fears, and some are related to judgments. Other blocks are related to assumed outcomes. In each case, there is a thought or belief that paralyzes you from standing up, walking over to the record player, and lifting the needle to make a change. Let's explore some of these blocks more closely.

Fear-based blocks are those things that strike terror in your heart, make your palms sweaty, or churn your stomach up full of butterflies. They focus you on the worst possible outcomes and the biggest potential losses. They shrewdly get into your head until you feel like what you fear is the absolute reality or truth of what will happen.

Blocks related to judgment are those that you create for yourself based either on how you judge yourself ("I could never do that"), how you judge others ("She is too narrow-minded to let me make a change for our family"), or how someone will judge you, which ties back to a fear ("I'll look stupid or incompetent.")

Another type of block may relate to your need to control an outcome. Sometimes this takes the shape of an unwillingness to let go of certainty, to make a change, and to face a result that can't be guaranteed. For example, you would love to have a different job, but you are too worried that if you move to a new position, you might not like it after all. This block is of the variety of "better the devil you know than the devil you don't," and means that it is often better to deal with someone or something you are familiar with and know, even if they are not ideal, than take a risk with an unknown person, thing, or situation.

Then, there is the terrible habit we sometimes have of presuming that we know an outcome when we really don't ("I don't need to ask her. I already know what she's going to say.") We get it so set in our minds that we *know* how something will turn out (negatively, of course), that we limit ourselves from taking action.

What's the Truth?

That last block makes me think of a client of mine, Steve, who worked as a VP for a popular sports magazine. He worked in the communications department, and he had a wonderful relationship with the CEO of the company. Steve knew he was doing well there, but at that time the company was going through some layoffs. After reaching out to the CEO a few times to see what was going on, he still hadn't received any return emails or calls from him and he began to worry.

At our next coaching session, Steve still hadn't heard from the CEO. He expressed how odd it was that he didn't hear back from him and it had to mean he was getting canned. As a result of this "truth," Steve was angry and disheartened and had started to slack off a little at work, coming ill-prepared to a meeting and doing a shoddy job on a presentation. When I probed these behaviors, he replied, "What's the point? I'm getting fired so why should I give them my best efforts? It won't mean anything anyway."

It was then that I employed an old technique used for creating possibilities where it seemed none existed. I started by turning his belief that he was going to be fired from being the only outcome to being simply one possibility. "Okay, that's one possibility," I told him. Then I had Steve come up with about ten different creative scenarios as to why the CEO might not have returned his calls. Some of the more interesting examples he came up with were that the CEO's phone was broken, he was getting his molars removed and couldn't speak, or his dog died and he just couldn't face him. On we went, making up all kinds of reasons (funny, sad, dramatic, mean, unlikely, etc.) for why he hadn't heard back from him.

Then I asked Steve what the craziest reason in the world might have been. He chuckled sarcastically and said, "Oh, because I'm getting a promotion and a raise and he felt awkward telling me this in the middle of these layoffs."

After giving my client a minute or two to reflect on his varied responses, I asked him which one of them was the real reason. He still believed he was getting fired, but he realized that he had created that possibility just as he had made up all of those other crazy scenarios. We talked more about what he could do to ensure that his work, and ultimately his reputation, didn't suffer. We also prepared contingencies in the event he did get laid off. As we hung up the phone to end our coaching session, he was armed with a newly empowered perspective and an action plan.

A few days later he called me back and said, "I was right!" I waited for the punch line. Nothing. "Go on . . ." I pleaded. He said with a mix of astonishment and excitement, "I got a promotion and a raise." Really.

Sometimes we feel like we know what an outcome will be. We have an entire scene played out in our heads, and we believe without any doubt that real life is going to mirror what we've created in our minds. Sometimes it does. Sometimes our belief actually causes it to happen (i.e., self-fulfilling prophecy like if Steve was fired for his shoddy work). Sometimes none of it may be true.

Your mission is to challenge yourself to identify where you are blocked behind a belief that seems like the truth. Know that whatever scenario you're making up is just one possible outcome. Prepare for it so it stings less if it happens, but don't get stuck there. Stay empowered and make up different endings to that story, so you can stay engaged along the way. Who knows? Maybe you're going to get a promotion and a raise . . .

Kids, Please Try This at Home

Here's a short exercise so you can experience what my client did in the example above.

Identify a situation you are currently facing where you believe that you "already know" what the outcome is going to be.

1) Write down ten alternative outcomes. Really play here—the crazier the better.

2) Develop a contingency plan so you are prepared if the negative outcome occurs, but don't get stuck there.

3) Choose the best possible outcome as "the truth." Really step into it as if that is the one that is destined to happen. Note any changes in your mood, your energy, your behaviors, and your levels of stress and fear.

4) Once the situation has resolved, revisit this exercise and write down what actually occurred. What did you learn from this experience? Where else in your life can you apply this new learning?

These Blocks Are at Your Service

Are you starting to get a sense of what those things are that are blocking your own progress in your life or business? Now that we are identifying and naming them, how do they make you feel? Angry? Stressed? Resentful? Something else?

Listen, we all have blocks. They are one of the ways we protect ourselves from getting hurt, feeling pain, or experiencing stress. Remember the earlier section in Chapter 3 on the excuse machine? One of my excuses—or blocks—was to tell myself I wasn't interested in something. In reality, I *was* interested, but I was worried that if I pursued that activity, I'd fail and be judged for it. So I protected myself from risking that outcome by throwing up a block: "I'm not interested in that!" and that's how I acted.

Noah Blumenthal, known as one of the Top 100 Minds on Personal Development by *Leadership Excellence* magazine, agrees that our behaviors are driven by the rewards they provide. "These rewards . . . encourage you to perpetuate your current behavior." For example, if you tend to become defensive, Blumenthal suggests, "You may fear that your actions will be viewed as ignorant or stupid. Your defensiveness helps you justify your actions and protects you from being wrong."[2]

It helps once you realize what a block really is—not a weakness or a shortcoming—but a device you use to keep yourself protected. Once you understand that concept, you can begin to get beyond the block—rather than getting stuck behind it—and see what's really making it difficult for you to make a change. With this access you can then choose to change, influence, or accept it. Once I discovered what was hiding beneath my "I'm not interested" block—which was actually, "I don't want to look foolish or incompetent"—I could create a plan for getting past it.

My friend Suzanne has a block that many people share—fear of speaking in front of a group. When we probed what lay beneath that block, she realized that she was afraid of making a mistake and being seen as inadequate. As we continued to dig a little deeper, it became clear that her block is not really a fear of speaking, but a fear of being unprepared and looking bad, causing others to be disappointed in her.

With this access, we were able to come up with a few tactical ideas to help her get past it. (Note that we didn't delve into the psychology of the block but rather how it hindered her actions and affected her confidence.) Our plan included for her to do more preparation prior to a presentation so she was sure she knew her stuff cold before giving a talk, including creating opportunities to role-play so she could see that she could survive giving the talk. We strategized ways she could start with a smaller, less intimidating group. We even determined the value of making sure she's well rested, hydrated, and in peak physical condition before her talk. So that had the added benefit of sparking her in her commitment to exercising as well.

Once we recognize our blocks and how they are trying to protect us, we can let go of the resistance and judgment we have for certain activities, opening up all kinds of possible things we can do to minimize the block and to allow ourselves to step over it, into a new reality. That's disruption at its best.

Conclusion

What are the things you are doing every day that may need to be disrupted for you to be able to move closer to your extraordinary life? Is it time to disrupt long nights at work without having dinner with the family? Is it time to disrupt your habit of eating out several nights a week so you can instead put more money in the bank or lose the pounds that have been bugging you for years? Is it time to disrupt your routine of watching TV at night so you can get to bed earlier and wake earlier to hit the gym? If you're going to start living your extraordinary life, you have to be able to break out of the old routines and create new ones. You must master the art of disruption, even if it means pulling into the neighbor's driveway from time to time!

You are sure to find some blocks along the way as you try to disrupt, break out, and break through your old way of doing things. Maybe you are a mastermind at creating excuses because you are afraid, maybe you worry that your new life won't be as good as your old one, or maybe you tell yourself you aren't smart or creative or disciplined enough to create a new routine, or maybe you don't believe disrupting your routine will have any benefit at all so why bother?

That's understandable. You don't want to get hurt or become *more* unhappy than you might be now—and these blocks are trying to "protect" you from that. It's true that they may even be safeguarding you from certain pain or discomfort. But in the process, what is also happening? Are you getting boxed into a life that is only . . . fine? I already know that if you've gotten this far in this book, you are no longer willing to settle for fine. I know I'm not willing to settle for fine. I've seen fine and it isn't nearly as much fun as extraordinary.

If you are ready to join me on the path to extraordinary, take some time to familiarize yourself with your blocks. Recognize where and when and how they are helping you. Thank them for their efforts, then kindly dismantle them, put them in a box, or send them on their way. When you try to disrupt things without these blocks, you may still feel fear; you may still feel afraid. That's okay. As others have said before, courage is being afraid and doing something anyway.

Are you ready to trust and try something new? Are you ready to disrupt the old patterns and see how far you can go when you do something differently? If you are willing, your extraordinary, perfectly designed life awaits.

PURPOSE

"It's a terrible thing to see and have no vision."
~ Helen Keller

5

Don't Let Life Just Happen to You

"In this age, which believes that there is a short cut to everything, the greatest lesson to be learned is that the most difficult way is, in the long run, the easiest."

~Henry Miller

I have an important question for you. In your life right now, are you heading toward a specific *and desired* destination, or are you just sort of floating down the river to wherever the currents seem to take you?

If you're like most of us, you have a very busy life and you are doing a lot every day. But are you doing the things that will move you closer to *where you want to be*? And where do you really want to be, anyway? If you don't know where it is you want to go, how can you possibly get there?

If you sometimes feel like you're expending lots of energy without actually moving toward something—or toward something that you really want—you're not alone. Many of my clients are in the same situation—and I was there too before September 11th, 2001.

When I speak to audiences about rewriting their future, I sometimes share the following excerpt from *Alice in Wonderland*, where Alice happens upon the Cheshire Cat.

"Would you tell me, please, which way I ought to go from here?"

"That depends a good deal on where you want to get to," said the Cat.

"I don't much care where—" said Alice.

"Then it doesn't matter which way you go," said the Cat.

"—so long as I get SOMEWHERE," Alice added as an explanation.

"Oh, you're sure to do that," said the Cat, "if you only walk long enough."

Are you living just like Alice? If you have no plan and no direction for your life, you may live your day-to-day existence without really heading anywhere at all. You *want* to get somewhere—but if you don't know where that is or how to get there, you may be exerting plenty of energy without actually making any progress.

That is not to say that you're not happy or even thrilled with certain aspects of your life. What I am referring to is whether or not you wrote the script for this movie called "Your Life" that you are starring in each day. Or is it someone else's script? Is it the movie you want to make? In his book, *The Four Agreements*, author Don Miguel Ruiz, an Indian Shaman, defines the life that we are living as a dream of our own creation. Is your life the dream you want to live?

This section of the book is dedicated to helping you uncover that amazing destination. That's why in Chapter 8, we will work together to uncover your vision for your life. But let's begin first, in this chapter, with discovering the blocks that are stopping you from naming that vision or even dreaming. We will then take a little "rest stop" in Chapter 6 to make sure that you don't lose sight of where you are today—it's important to get the most out of the present while you are moving toward the future. If you forget to be present in the present, you may end up sabotaging the very people, places, and responsibilities that you need to usher you toward your future (hey, like a paying job!) Then, we will gear up for creating your vision with a chapter on core values (Chapter 7). We want you to be crystal clear on what these are so you can create a vision that's aligned with the things that are most important to you.

Having a clear vision for our lives is a crucial step in designing and living an extraordinary life. However, most of us never take the time to figure out where we want to go. What would happen if you began to live your life with intention and purpose? What if instead of just going where the river takes you, you live *into* a vision that you've created for yourself?

Floating down the river is no longer a luxury you can afford. Letting life just happen to you simply won't cut it. I don't want you to be like Alice, unclear on where you are going. I don't want you to give away your power to external forces or people. Instead, I want you to live your life full of intention and full of hope toward a future that you've designed and are striving for. You deserve that (and more), and this chapter and section of the book can help inspire you to go get it.

Floating Down the River

I know firsthand what it's like to live a life without intention, clear purpose, or direction. Let me explain.

Growing up, I considered myself one of the lucky ones—I was raised in a loving home, did well in school, was a good athlete, and always had a girlfriend. I let my life go wherever it took me and that seemed to work out fine. Doing this is what I now call floating down the river. Until recently, I was a master at it.

Like some young adults, I never really knew what I wanted to do, and I never really made a lot of active choices. I just dealt with things as they showed up and came my way. I did some good things and met a lot of good people, but my work really wasn't fulfilling. I was stuck and I didn't even know it. I just felt that I had no direction.

For a long time, I didn't realize the eventual cost of all of this reactive living. By foregoing much of the say in my own life's direction, I put my course in the hands of the currents, naïve to the need to take the oars. Funny how that works—here I was enjoying how "easy" my life was, not realizing how unprepared I was and how hard just floating down the river was going to make things later.

My first full-time job was in retirement benefits administration. Say it with me . . . *Retirement-Benefits-Administration*. I was twenty-two years old, and retirement was about the farthest thing from my mind. However, I was enamored with the earnings potential and didn't really think about the fact that I might have to "work hard" to earn my living.

I learned fast. After seven tedious months, I had had enough. I was uninspired, bored, lost, and miserable. I made one of my first executive decisions—I would quit. Did I have another opportunity lined up? Not even a bite. Did I consider the ramifications of trying to find a job as a recent college graduate in the recessional economy of 1990? Not at all. Hey, I was making a big decision. Wasn't that enough?

I walked right into my boss's office and before I could even begin my semi-rehearsed remarks, he fired me. I just sat there in a stupor, hearing something to the effect of "Blah blah . . . . you're a smart kid . . . blah blah . . . not a good fit . . . blah blah . . . you'll be fine . . . blah blah."

Then I heard, "WAKE UP!" as my boss raised his volume to awaken me out of my funk. That startled me and brought me back to the reality of now being officially jobless and not having a backup plan. That was the first time I felt the cost of my career apathy.

I stayed in this career rut for many years, floating through other companies—some corporate, some entrepreneurial. I met truly wonderful people, yet the work itself never really fit me well. Days weren't bad—they were fine—and I had plenty of good days to go along with the mediocre ones. However, from a career perspective, none of them provided me with the meaning that I was craving.

One of my biggest problems was that I had no vision for my life. I didn't know where I wanted to go or how to begin. So I did what most of us do . . . nothing. Time kept melting away, and days became months, which soon added up to years.

Some of you may know the drill:

> Get up early, breakfast on the run, train to the city, subway downtown, long workday, subway uptown, train back home, late dinner, get to bed because you have to wake up early, and then the next morning, do it all over again. Your work feels unimportant—maybe you even feel out of place—and you just start wishing away the days until it's the weekend or a vacation.

I didn't know what to do to fix my discontent, but one day, I fully realized that I had to stop "losing days." That was September 10th and you already know that story. By listening to my inner instinct about the kind of life I really wanted for myself, I managed to save my life—not only figuratively, but literally. That simple mental picture on September 10th of having breakfast with my family will always remain an incredible reminder to me of how powerful it can be to have a vision for one's life—and what can occur when you set an intention and follow through on it.

What Stops Us

What stops us from creating a vision for our lives? Why is it so hard to create one? From personal experience and working with thousands of people, I believe there are a handful of factors at play here, which I will introduce here and address further in the coming chapters. Think about each of the following and see how each may apply to your life.

#1: We haven't taken an honest look at where we are today. How satisfied are you with the various areas of your life? When is the last time you really assessed your happiness and satisfaction with each of them? I'm not speaking of the occasional or even daily complaining. To me, that is just a pressure valve that lets the ever-building steam out. I'm referring to a productive and honest look at your life. If you haven't taken the time to reflect on how you truly feel about your life today and what you'd like it to look like tomorrow, you won't have the insight you need to develop a vision for what you really want.

#2: We aren't tightly connected to our core values (or what's important to us). We all have a sense of morals and values that we live by. These values provide us with guidelines for how we want to live our lives and are the pillars of our being. How aligned are your behaviors and your values? When you are not living your day-to-day life in a way that is connected to these values or you can't see a way to make that happen, it is difficult to create a meaningful vision.

#3: We are unsure of our sense of purpose (what we stand for). Who are you? Why are you here? What are you meant to do or be in this world? How aware are you of your own nature or essence? How do you even define "life purpose"? Trying to answer these big questions can be uncomfortable, even overwhelming. But they are an important ingredient in creating your vision, as your sense of purpose makes your vision meaningful, exciting, and inspiring.

#4: We focus on HOW instead of WHAT. We are so concerned with "how" we are going to do something that we don't even let ourselves dream anymore. Many times we simply squash our thoughts

and our dreams before we allow them to breathe. An idea comes up and we immediately try to figure out if it's achievable and how we will accomplish it. If we don't have an instant solution, we dismiss our thoughts and ideas as silly, unrealistic, too hard, or even impossible.

"I can't make a living doing that." "That will never happen for me." "I can't do that." It's like that Whack-a-Mole game at the arcade. You know the one where the mole pops out of the hole and we have to bonk it on the head before it goes back down? Those are our dreams popping up and there we are, waiting to whack them in the head and knock them back down to the ground (except there's no big stuffed animal prize waiting for you here).

#5: *We'll do it "tomorrow."* This is another byproduct of the "hangover" I referred to in Chapter 1, and it is a huge vision killer. Our constant need to provide instant responses to everything and receive instant gratification makes it increasingly more difficult to find time for activities that require thoughtfulness and deeper thinking. We say to ourselves, "Not now. I don't have the time, money, or energy." Instead, we believe that *someday* we'll do it—one day, when the kids are older, or when we have more money or more time . . . or when life is not so hectic. (The reality is that *someday* will never come.) As a result, we get stuck in reactive mode because we're so "busy" and days continue to slip by.

#6: *Yeah, but . . . (all the reasons why you can't).* This takes us back to the excuse machine. When I ask my clients to start crafting a vision, it's amazing how these blocks start to show up. They don't even let themselves dream—whether they're trying to prevent themselves from certain disappointment, or they're defining all that's really possible from their slice of life experience, or the concept of doing something differently or playing bigger scares the heck out of them. Either way, they are stuck in their minds and can't see a way to expand their vision beyond their current thoughts.

No matter the reason, floating down the river will keep you in a life that is uninspired, misaligned, or just fine. None of these outcomes are acceptable, are they? I don't think so, and I doubt that you do either. How about aiming instead for a life that is filled with meaning and purpose? In the next chapter, that's where you can begin to shift your energies.

Conclusion

According to Hyrum W. Smith in his book *The 10 Natural Laws of Successful Time and Life Management*, only three percent of us ever do any kind of life planning. *Three percent!* For much of my own life, I just floated down the river, letting the circumstances of my life steer, rather than really planning and taking the initiative. Without a sense of where I wanted to go, I just dealt with whatever showed up and came my way. Like I said, no vision.

The good news is that painting a picture of your future is entirely up to you. This is not the kind of thing you can rely on someone else to create for you—but that's okay, because who wants someone else's vision for your life? This needs to come from inside of you.

So many of us live our lives just like Alice in Wonderland, not really knowing where we want to go. As we saw in the beginning of this chapter, when Alice came upon the Cheshire Cat, the cat asserted that if Alice didn't care where she wanted to go, it didn't much matter which way she went after all.

I'm sure you will agree with me that where you go in your life does matter quite a bit. It matters to your happiness and your sense of life satisfaction. It matters, too, to the happiness of your friends and family, who will benefit from the positivity you bring into the world while you are out there really living.

You deserve to live a brilliant and extraordinary life—one that has you living out your greatest potential and enjoying your life, your work, your activities, and your community every step of the way. In the next chapter, we will focus on what will bring your life that meaning . . . not *someday*, but today.

6

Make the Most of It

"Do all the good you can. By all the means you can. In all the ways you can. In all the places you can. To all the people you can. As long as ever you can."

~John Wesley

It's no small deal to create and move into your life vision. Hey, we're talking about designing your dream life here. It's bigger! It's better! Can't you already feel yourself getting excited? Don't you just want to throw all of your resources at it?

But wait a minute. Don't forget about your existing life—you know, the one you've been living up until now, the one that pays the bills and keeps the home front running.

While you are starting to work toward your future and you are getting more and more excited about your tomorrow, let's see how we can also make the present great rather than falling into the temptation to disengage and allow things to come apart. Let's make the most of where you are, not sabotage it.

Chances are, you will be living your current life for a while longer. Chances are, you may not be able to bound out of your current situation right away. It will take time and exploration, time and actions, time and refinement to move into your new life. In the meantime, how are you going to get the most meaning from your current situation? Where you are today may not match your ideal, but it doesn't have to be a prison sentence or a miserable or even mediocre place.

Since real change involves a process and can't be acquired through a little blue pill, we will spend time in this chapter looking at how you can get the most meaning from your current situation while you are working on designing and developing the future that you want to live into. You may be super-motivated to jump into the next big thing in your life, but if that isn't possible—or wise—I want you to enjoy the process of getting there. When I became a coach, it took me three years to get to the point where I owned my own successful business, and I suspect it might take you some time to build your own extraordinary life too. So let's look at how you can shift into a life of meaning today, even before you make any grand or sweeping changes or while you are in-process.

Why Bother?

On September 10, when I went back to my office after making the decision to have breakfast with my family the next morning, something interesting happened. My work went from blah to good. It wasn't the work itself that had changed; it was my relationship to my work that had changed. I realized how much I was making myself suffer and how I was blaming the company for how I was feeling. But after taking back control of my life with that small decision to have breakfast with my family, I was able to let go of all of that resentment and re-engage my responsibilities at my current job. After all, the Company hadn't done anything wrong except to pay me a good salary to do my job. I had to shift from judgment to gratitude—and when I did, it changed everything.

I knew I wanted to ultimately find something that was more meaningful for me in terms of career, but I didn't have the vision of what that was yet, so I made the most of my current situation while I was still in it. I led a fantastic team and launched important programs and products, and my work consistently received positive reviews. This allowed me to stay in a positive mindset and keep up my energy level while I contemplated my next move.

Whether you find that you are dissatisfied, in an unstable situation, or primed for something different, I encourage you to focus on maximizing your current situation so you can be in the best shape you can be to make a change. It's never good to take on the challenge of making a life change from a place of desperation.

What do we do when we are feeling desperate? We are more likely to jump on the next boat to "Anywhere Else" just because it takes us away from wherever our "Here" happens to be. But remember, to create an extraordinary life you aren't going to jump into any old boat and float down any old river. Instead, you are going to envision what kind of boat you want to be on (sailboat? speedboat? cruise liner to the tropics?). You are also going to envision which body of water you'd really enjoy navigating, and in which destination you really want to end up.

Instead of making any drastic or desperate moves, I want you to stabilize your current situation first while you design your extraordinary life and all it will entail. Our goal will be to help you maximize your current experience so you can carve out time to think about the future. Re-engaging and trying to maximize your current experience while setting up a life change has its benefits. For example, while living your present life, you can still:

- maintain some stability of income
- learn something where you are

- develop new skills
- network and make important connections for later
- keep your performance strong to maintain your confidence
- try to enjoy each day as much as possible—these days still count!

There are many more benefits that you will likely discover, unique to your own situation, when you just take the time to reflect. As you begin to trust the process of change and have faith that you will find your way to your extraordinary future, you may discover, like me, that you can do the same work for a time and yet view it differently. If you can find meaning within your present situation—for example, gratitude for a job that provides you the funds needed to attend school at night—you will unlock valuable energy and creativity to apply to designing your extraordinary future.

How to Get There: Maximizing Your Current Experience

I want to share with you my three favorite methods for getting the most out of your current experience.

First, I want you to avoid the sabotage trap. This means doing the right thing—bringing respect and responsibility to your present situation rather than simply mentally abandoning it or intentionally damaging it. Basically, you don't want to check out or screw up in your present life. You want to make a change when *you* are ready . . . not because your actions cause others to eject you.

Second, experiment with adding a new understanding to your current situation—uncovering its larger meaning. By digging deeper, you may realize that what you are doing right now does have purpose and that by staying connected to this purpose you can regain new energy or motivation. You may also be able to find meaning in your situation by adding in a new activity, as you will see one of my colleagues managed to do.

Lastly, focus on how you can *be* in a situation. Regardless of the work you do or the tasks and responsibilities that fill your day—no matter how mundane or mismatched with your personality and interests—you always have the freedom to bring those activities to life through your mindset and your interactions. As a result, you can bring meaning to a situation not just by what you do but by the way you interact with others—through your way of being. Let's take a closer look at each of these three methods more closely.

Avoid the sabotage trap. When you're unhappy with a certain aspect of your life, how do you respond? Do you feel powerless to affect change? Do you grin and bear it? Some people go even further and make the situation worse by sabotaging it. I am talking about the things you will be tempted to do when you stop caring—like showing up late to meetings, blowing off your diet, starting fights with your partner, not preparing for a presentation, etc. You may find yourself sabotaging a situation just to force your own or someone else's hand. In other words, you make things so bad that a change has to happen. But is it the change you want or need, and is that change really on your own terms?

You don't have to sabotage your happiness or success so that you create enough urgency to force change. When I was younger, being the "nice guy" that I was, I hated breaking up with a girlfriend. So I would disengage from the relationship and make it unpleasant enough so that she would break up with me. Obviously, I still had a lot of growth in front of me. When I look back, I see that I was trying to cause an outcome by putting it in someone else's hands instead of being accountable for doing it myself.

I find many people do the exact same thing. In their work, they check out and disengage when they no longer want to be where they are. Maybe they're afraid that if work gets to be okay or even good, they'll get complacent and get trapped there. So they feel they have to make sure they're miserable enough to keep the "I need to get the heck out of here" conversation alive in their heads.

What a wasted opportunity that is! When I find that kind of sabotage going on with one of my clients, we completely recreate the conversation. First, we re-engage with the reality that they are in command. They are choosing to stay where they are and they can choose to leave, regardless of how compelling their "success" may be (in terms of pay, prestige, or otherwise). Once they get clear that they'll be able to choose to leave no matter how much happiness or success they are experiencing, they give up their saboteur mentality.

Next, we look at what they can do to make the most of it. How can they see it as an opportunity to suck as much knowledge and experience from the situation as possible while they are there? Who can they network with? What skills can they develop or refine? Etc. That gives them the ability to leave on their own terms when they are truly prepared and ready.

In the end, it is always better to make a change on your own terms. Avoiding the sabotage trap will allow you to retain more control and power as you plan your transition.

Find the meaning. Now that we know you're not going to do something irrational or irreparable to sabotage your present situation (see how smart you're becoming?!), you are ready to take on this next very cool challenge of finding the meaning in your present situation. Sometimes it's easy to find the meaning but sometimes you have to work a little to create it. Meaning was missing in almost every job I ever had. In fact, when I started my job at the World Trade Center, I didn't even know what the company did. I was hired by an acquaintance from another job.

It turns out that the company was in the insurance business. How was I going to find meaning in insurance? I can hear some of you saying, "Insurance brokerage—that's sounds pretty interesting," and that's absolutely perfect because meaning and interest are in the eye of the beholder, after all. But that wasn't how I felt at the time.

At this new job, a colleague who was a bit older than me saw that I didn't have much knowledge of the insurance industry. He was one of those very warm and caring people. He was also what I'd call a "teacher"—everything about him signaled that teaching was his gift—his nature. As a result, he offered to teach another woman and me the basics of risk management and insurance. At first, I was hesitant because I had absolutely no interest in the topic; but he insisted so I went along with him. Every Tuesday, the three of us would go downstairs and have lunch outside together and my colleague would hold class. We had textbooks and everything! He even assigned us homework.

Within the first two weeks, I started to understand the role and value insurance played for companies. If you don't manage your risk, you're not in business.

As a company, we were the best in helping people manage those risks. So now, all of a sudden, I could understand the value of my work—I could assign some meaning to it. My friend increased the depth of meaning in his work by taking us on as students. He created this meaning on his own. Nobody asked him to teach us, and he wasn't getting any credit for it. He just wanted to.

My colleague was a good man, and the other woman who sat in on our "classes" was a really happy, generous, and warm young lady. They were good people. September 11th was going to be our fifth class together, but neither of them made it out of the building that day. I often look back and think about both of them with gratitude and a smile. My friend understood the value of his work, and it was easy for him to create meaning around it. I, on the other hand, had to work a little bit to create meaning for myself. Once I did, it made a huge impact for me.

Where can you find meaning in your current situation? Is there a new activity you can add to the mix, like my colleague who chose to teach others, which will bring your work to life? This applies to unpaid work and activities too—from daily responsibilities to weekly tasks. Maybe it's just taking the time to connect the dots between what you're already doing and its positive effect in the world. Who can you mentor or take under your wing? Do you want a mentor for yourself?

What if we apply this idea of finding meaning to a relationship? Let's say you and your spouse have drifted apart and you don't see a future for you as a couple. However, you are not ready to split up . . . that's a big move after all. Finances are tight and you're not ready to disclose the problems in your marriage to your children, your family, or your friends. How can you make the most out of your current situation so that you and your family's suffering are minimized? In other words, what meaning or motivation can you employ while you remain in the relationship?

Perhaps it's a commitment to being civil and not fighting or bad-mouthing each other in front of the kids. Maybe it's finding a new activity that fulfills you (tennis, painting, martial arts) or one in which you can make new friends. Maybe it's making a commitment to go to a marriage counselor to see if you and your spouse can reconnect. The idea is not to be miserable or make this situation untenable. Rather, since you're choosing to stay, then you must find a way to re-engage the relationship as you work out what your next step will be.

As we will see in the next section, sometimes you can find meaning by being who you want to be in a situation without changing the activities at all.

It's who you are being, not what you are doing. One of the keys to being able to maximize the meaning in your current situation has to do with the concept of *being versus doing*. I am reminded of a parking attendant I once knew who had the most amazing presence in spite of his totally unglamorous job. Let me explain . . .

Years ago, I occasionally had to go up to Hartford, Connecticut, to facilitate all-day training classes for my company. It was about an hour's drive from my house so I'd just hop in my car and drive up there. The parking lot was down underneath the building, and it was a dark and dank environment, where the smell of exhaust mingled with every breath. Like many places, you would take a ticket that tracked your hours, and at the end of the day you'd pull up to a small booth, give the parking attendant your four dollars, and you'd be on your way. Of course, there was always a long line of cars waiting to pay so you'd sit there idling in the exhaust that you were helping to create, waiting for the "warden" to take your money and pardon you so you could be free.

I had been training people all day long so I was wiped out, a little cranky, a little hungry, and not looking forward to the hour-long drive home. I couldn't wait until I was home relaxing on my couch. I pulled up to this booth to pay my parking ticket, I rolled down my window, and this booming voice almost shouted at me, "How are you doing today, my friend?" The mix of energy, positivity, and volume caught me completely by surprise. It woke me out of my tired funk immediately and I came to attention. I gave a tired smile and answered plainly, "Pretty good. How are you doing?" I wasn't sure what to expect next.

Keeping his energy levels and volume sustained, the parking attendant said to me, "My brother, I am doing great! I am alive, I am loved, I have a good job, and I get to meet good people like you all day long! What more can a man ask for?"

I thought about it for a second, nodded in agreement, gave him a simple "thanks," and started driving off, but he wasn't done and offered me a final, "No, thank *you*, my friend."

A few minutes later, after the shock wore off, I realized how blown away I was by this man. I mean, here's a guy sitting down in an exhaust-filled dungeon, dealing with uncaring, unhappy people all day long, and he was perhaps the happiest man I had ever met in my life. I thought about him all the way home and then thought about it for days. I had to go up to Hartford and do that training for a number of times over the next year, and every time I went up there, that parking attendant was my favorite part of the day. I never got his name, but I started to recognize him and would even look forward to paying for my parking ticket! It put me in a good mood just knowing I was going to be in the garage seeing this man. He never disappointed . . . he was the same joyful presence every time.

I would never have predicted that a parking attendant—doing menial work day after day in that sunless, odor-filled place—could be so happy and full of joy. Let's face it—what the parking attendant was doing was nothing to be excited about. He sat in a little box in a dark basement and he took parking tickets and money from people, giving them back change that had probably been touched by many hands. He would open the gate and then came another car with more fumes and reason to touch more worn and dirty money. This is what the parking attendant did *all day long*—not particularly exciting or appetizing, right?

But there he was, beaming and thanking me (and likely every other customer he saw that day). This man found his meaning by sharing a smile and spreading his positive energy to the many people who came his way each day. It wasn't about the specific work he was *doing* that contributed to his joyful voice and presence. It was about who he chose to *be* while performing his job.

It's always our choice to be a certain way. This parking attendant created that meaning every single day by being a source of positive energy for others. He still "talks" into my head once in a while. When I have to do something that I'm not really fond of, I think of him. Even though I don't know his name, he's influenced my life for the better, and now he's influenced all of you as well.

I am a big believer in the fact that we have a lot of influence over the way we spend our time. Life is ours to create. That being said, there may be times when we have to accept the reality of a less-than-pleasant situation until we can effect change or move on to something better. This is when being, rather than doing, can come into play.

In Japanese culture, one of the highest aims is to cultivate a spirit called "Kokoro Gamae." Although it is difficult to adequately translate the precise meaning of "Kokoro Gamae" from Japanese to English, according to Yoshie Sugai, the President of Japanese leadership development company SugaiLabo, "Someone who has Kokoro Gamae possesses 'a calm yet prepared heart, or spirit, who can take immediate and effective action in any situation.' The practice of the Japanese Martial Arts is a constant exercise in achieving this state of 'calm readiness.'"[3]

Who is it that you need to be in order to feel true to yourself and at peace in any given situation? Maybe you struggle to find the larger meaning in your work—how it connects and contributes to your life or to the larger world. Maybe there is something missing from a relationship—how it supports you in being your authentic, confident, and powerful self. Does the lack of an answer need to dis-empower or depress you? I don't think it has to. One of the best ways to take back the power in a situation is to be true to yourself by honoring your values through the way you act. This will look different for each person. Maybe it's natural for you to exude patience and gentleness; maybe your gift is friendliness and encouragement.

For some of you, this will be an easy, rattle-it-off answer. For others, it may take dusting off the cobwebs of a distant time when you used to know who you wanted to be. Or maybe this is one of the first times you've ever asked yourself this question! If so, let me reassure you that yes, you have the freedom to be whomever you want to be in the world—not the person your mother or father wanted you to be, not the person your friends or family members tried to shape you into, and not the person who has always done everything for everyone else. It's time to be your true self.

Once you start to dream of a future that is bigger and better for yourself—that is incredible and extraordinary—it is definitely possible that your present situation might start to feel or look a little drab. But wait! Remember the parking attendant who worked in that awful-seeming basement who thought he had a good job and who asked "What more can a man ask for?" It might seem like a stretch, but you can get there too. I promise.

Make the Most of Your Present

The following questions can be useful in determining where you are dissatisfied in your life and how you can maximize the current experience while you contemplate your next move.

- What is an area of your life that you are dissatisfied with and for which you want to make a change?
- For this area, where can you find meaning there? What value does it provide for you? For others? What new activities can you add to the mix to create more meaning?
- What words would others use to describe you? Is that how you'd like to be perceived? What needs to change to get your public persona more closely aligned with who you really are?
- How might you be sabotaging this situation (i.e., making it worse than it really is)? Where are you avoiding accountability or surrendering your power to either change, influence, or accept it?

Conclusion

Many times we let our resentments, disappointments, and judgments define how we experience our lives. Yet, we can still gain much value by shifting our mindset from one of tolerance and avoidance to one of accountability and intention.

First, don't give into the temptation to relax your standards and disengage your present life. Seek gratitude instead, discovering the benefits that your present situation offers you. Dig a little until you find the meaning. Where is the value in what you presently do? This will enable you to stay empowered and avoid the sabotage trap so you can design your next move from a place of confidence and power. You'll then be in the right mind frame to squeeze the most out of your current situation and reconnect to its larger meaning in a way that re-energizes you.

Second, remember that you can always, always, always bring your presence to a situation. Fulfillment comes not just from what you are doing but from who you are being. Eventually, you will make a plan for how to permanently shift into a life of *doing* what you love. But while you are in these early stages—exploring, envisioning, and creating a picture of the life you want and then planning for it—you can focus on embodying (being!) the person you want to be.

The next two chapters of the book will help you explore this question of who you want to be in great depth. As you reconnect with your core values in the next chapter, you will be able to live out your present reality with the fulfillment of being true to who you really are.

7

Don't Live Upside Down (Unless You're a Possum)

"Often people attempt to live their lives backwards: they try to have more things, or more money, in order to do more of what they want so that they will be happier. The way it actually works is the reverse. You must first be who you really are, then, do what you need to do, in order to have what you want."

~Margaret Young

To create a vision of the future, we want to start with the foundation, just like when we build a house. That foundation begins with defining our core values. When we're not living our day-to-day lives connected to those values, it's really difficult to create a meaningful vision.

How important are your spouse and your children to you? Replace "spouse" and "children" with anyone or anything you care about. Dumb question, I realize that. You know how important they are and you probably often verbalize it as well. However, do your actions support these values?

For me, it was the realization that my daughter was growing up seeing me only on weekends that really woke me up. Yes, it's easy to justify that my work was a priority. But so was my family. How could I be responsible with my job and be present in my family's life?

I started by thinking beyond binary. In other words, I didn't look at my decisions as either all or nothing. Instead, I looked for a small step that would allow me to take some control back. My choice was a twenty-minute breakfast during the workweek, so I could have a little awake-time with my daughter and stop the hamster-wheel pattern.

Is your small choice going to keep you out of harm's way like mine ultimately did? That's not the right question. A better one is—will your choice and subsequent action bring you closer to the life you *desire* to live? Will it create a small shift that brings your actions in closer alignment with your values?

In order to ensure that our behaviors are aligned with our core values, we need to determine what those values are. This chapter will define what I mean by core values and help to explain why these are so foundational to your ability to design and live an extraordinary life. You'll have an opportunity to define (or reconnect) with your own core values so that you gain this valuable insight into yourself.

What Are Core Values?

Your core values are the fundamental principles that reflect those things that are truly important to you. They define the way in which you want to live your life. These are not values that change from time to time or from situation to situation, but rather, they are the underpinning of you as a person and a human being. They're the pillars you can rely upon to help you make the "tough decisions" and guide your conduct in every interaction, every day. They are the foundation that you lean on when figuring out how to wrestle fears that are staring you right in the face! Your core values are the key components for designing a life that you love and feel fulfilled by.

My own core values are love, leadership, authenticity, and courage. I try to have these values lead me in everything I do. I don't always succeed at this, but having them defined sure helps me make decisions and act in ways that are more closely aligned with what's truly important to me. For example, when my two kids are fighting over which video game to play, my typical response is to yell (from wherever I am in the house), "If you don't stop fighting and figure it out, the TV goes off!" However, when I bring my core value of leadership to this milieu, I calmly help them figure out a way that's fair that they can do themselves next time.

It's a beautiful thing that each of us has our own unique core values. It's why we have doctors, teachers, artists, and a million other professions in the world. It's also why one doctor will be very different than another doctor, and why one teacher will have a totally different approach than another—not better, just different. When we replace judgment with appreciation, we see that this simply reflects the varied ways in which one person can contribute to the world versus another.

Why Identify Your Own Core Values?

Knowing what your core values are will give you the courage and the conviction needed to steer your own ship, even in stormy weather. Let me ask you this—what do you lean on when it comes time to make decisions? Are you crystal clear on what's important to you—on what's *really* important? Your core values can guide you in the difficult moments.

You may have to make challenging decisions to stay true to your core values. For example, will you accept the offer to take an important business trip to Europe or stay home to watch your child in the playoffs? Will you accept an invitation just for you to attend the U.S.

Tennis Open on the night of your spouse's birthday? Will you carve out time to volunteer at the local charity even though your calendar is full? These are the moments when you will be faced with a true test of character. However, you will have less drama and suffering if you know where you stand ahead of time. When you live your life by your core values, you won't have to second-guess your motives or your decisions. Knowing your core values offers all kinds of benefits.

When you have identified what your core values are, you will:

- gain real clarity about who you are and what you stand for
- make better choices about *where* you spend your time and *who* you spend it with
- overcome obstacles
- become more present
- prioritize your goals and stay focused on what matters most to you
- stay inspired and motivated
- be confident in your dreams.

For example, if one of your core values is service and you are presented with two competing job opportunities doing the same kind of work, but one for a nonprofit and one for a for profit organization, you can use your understanding of your core value of service to help predict which job would be more fulfilling to you, presumably the nonprofit. Of course, if financial security is a core value and the for-profit job pays more, you'll have to consider that issue as well. Ideally, you will look at your entire core-value picture—service, financial security, and all of your other values too—to come up with the right choice for you.

The key is to use your core values to generate your actions, which may not be your usual way of dealing with a situation. In other words, choose to honor your core values—and gain the motivation/courage/

inspiration you need to disrupt the status quo that's keeping you stuck in a life that's fine.

Identify Your Own Core Values

In identifying your core values, the best way that I have found to get started is to look at other people first. Think about three people who you admire or inspire you. What is it about them that calls to you, that you respect? It doesn't matter who they are—they could be alive, dead, real, fictional, movie or book characters, anyone. They could even be historical or mythical figures. It doesn't matter. Just make a list of those qualities that resonate the most with you.

For example, you may have a friend who speaks his mind freely and authentically and can communicate with anyone about anything without fear of consequence or judgment. Seeing him do this, you wish you could be as "out there" and self-expressed as he is. What are some of the core values your friend is demonstrating? Authenticity? Self-expression? Courage? Which ones are the most important to you? Which, if any, do you believe you'll never achieve but wish you could?

Here's the interesting part—as people, we tend to admire in others what we relate to most; what we want for ourselves. We wouldn't recognize these qualities in others unless they already existed within ourselves—even those that you feel are beyond your reach. There is an aspect of them that already exists inside of you.

The following exercise can be used to identify your own core values.

Define Your Core Values—Part I

Review the list of core values below and use it as a starting point for brainstorming your top five core values. You may see your values here, or you may think of new ones as you read this list. Write down your core values for future reference.

Truth	Creativity	Strength	Authenticity	Play
Peace	Courage	Dignity	Accountability	Love
Honor	Integrity	Loyalty	Flexibility	Security
Commitment	Fun	Persistence	Learning	Ease
Fairness	Faith	Spirituality	Honesty	Cooperation
Order	Collaboration	Respect	Dependability	Humor
Excellence	Adventure	Service	Trust	Freedom
Friendship	Caring	Connectedness	Steadiness	Kindness
Compassion	Dedication	Beauty	Generosity	Contribution
Optimism	Groundedness	Perseverance	Family	Resilience

This list of core values is just a starting point—a way for you to start brainstorming about your own. You can also complete Part II of this exercise to focus in on your unique core values.

Defining Your Core Values—Part II

1. Write down three people who you admire or who inspire you and state what it is about them that you respect (e.g., Gandhi: love, authenticity, peace). List all of their admirable qualities.

2. What you admire in others is a value you also hold for yourself. So, from the list you've just generated, choose between two and four core values to start with that either resonate for you the most or that you want to start with for yourself. Don't get hung up on making your choices—you can change them at any time. What's most important now is that you try these on—see if they fit you. They should empower you, excite you, and motivate you. They may even scare you just a little bit.

3. Once you have identified the ones that fit you best, write them down and put them in a place where you can see them often—such as in your calendar or journal or perhaps in the kitchen or in your office. What's important is that you start reinforcing what you have discovered about yourself and become more comfortable with the fit of the ones you choose. Again, if one is starting to feel not quite right, revisit the list and see if there is one that suits you better.

Living Aligned With Your Core Values

Now that you have started to define a few of your core values (you can change any of them at any time if they are not resonating with you), start to take a look at where your life is aligned or misaligned with them.

For example, if your core values include family, love, and courage, are you defining your life around those principles? Have you summoned the courage to define boundaries regarding your schedule to ensure you spend a certain amount of your time with your family?

If your core values include contribution and fun, what activities are you doing, either professionally or outside of work that support these values? Can you train for a 5k run to benefit your local community? Volunteer at a fundraising event? Give a free talk on a subject you know really well to those who can benefit from it, just to give a little something back? These are your *core values*, what you stand for in this life. If you are not supporting them with your actions (or, minimally, your intentions) you are living inauthentically.

When you look back upon your life, you will see periods where things were up and where they were down, where your fortunes were high and low. The true test of character is who you were being during all of those times and how you grew from the challenges you have faced. Your core values can guide you through these moments in time. After time has passed and your perspective shifts into one of reflection, you can look back with confidence and pride in knowing that you lived a life true to your values.

Conclusion

As you get more in tune with your core values and how they are reflected (or not) in your decisions and behaviors, you will gain the ability to use them as guides in everything you do. For example, if your core values are courage and authenticity, you can start to be more courageous and more authentic in all of the many areas of your life.

Doing this consistently day after day, and allowing yourself the bumps and bruises that come along with the process, will strengthen your connection to your own values and center your actions around those things that are most important to you, allowing you to live by them each day, authentically and on your terms.

8

Design a Future You Want to Live Into

"No one can go back and make a brand new start, my friend; but anyone can start from here and make a brand-new end."

~Dan Zadra

If I could start this chapter with a drum roll, I would. Why? It's time to get started! It's time to get creative. This is the moment you've all been waiting for. Drum roll, please . . .

What will your extraordinary life look like???

This simple question—and the answer—will change your life. So push the fears and worries aside and box up the insecurities and "what if's." This is your time to dream. This is your time to imagine and ask for it all. Why not, when anything's possible?

For some of you, you can easily paint a picture of what an ideal future would look like for one or more parts of your life. For you, we'll start there and break it down into the various pieces, or elements, that comprise it. For others, it may be difficult to start with a complete picture of the future. In your case, we take the opposite approach and start by identifying the elements that will ultimately form into a clear vision.

We begin the chapter by exploring what a life vision is. Then, you will have plenty of space and time to create your own.

The time has finally come to design your extraordinary life. Are you ready to get started?

What Is a Vision?

Let's begin with the vision. What is a vision anyway? Stated simply, a vision is a picture of your ideal future. It is like a painting of what you want your life to look like tomorrow, next month, or in five years. Thus, your vision can describe your short-term, medium-term, or long-term future—hopefully, all three. In fact, I encourage my clients to do short-term planning *and* long-term planning so they have tangible and exciting goals to focus on *now* and other more lofty goals to move toward in the future.

Let's start with an introspective exercise that will help you connect with your dreams and desires and see what you really want for your future. Remember, that future is already out there. It's just waiting for you to discover it.

In this exercise, I want you to step into an imaginary time machine and fast-forward to five years from now. It's important for you to know that in the five years that have passed, you were given everything you possibly needed to create the life you desired—ample time, sufficient money, necessary skills and training, and so on. You are now living *that life*—walking day-to-day through the amazing experience you have always wanted for yourself.

What does it look like? How do you spend your time each day? If you work, what does your job or career look like? Where do you live? What kind of friendships and family time do you enjoy? What else is going on that makes you feel alive and happy? Really see yourself in this future life. Smell the smells, breathe the air, and hear the sounds. Now shut your eyes for a minute and let your mind experience these things. Go ahead—I'll wait. When you are done enjoying this extraordinary life, step back into the time machine and return to today.

As you return back to the present timeframe, let's look at what you found. Were you able to paint a picture of that amazing future life? If so, where were you? What were you doing? Who were you with? What was the promise of that extraordinary-day-in-the-life that was waiting for you?

For those of you who were able to create a picture of your beautiful life five years from now, congratulations! You have just met your future. And guess what? It's not going anywhere. If you weren't able to do so or if some parts were cloudy, congratulations too! You've just found an area to focus on when developing your vision. You now have valuable guide posts that will help you get to the right answers for you.

Now that you've gotten a taste of your own vision for your life, let's spend a little more time exploring what a vision is so you have the understanding you need to create your own.

The elements of your vision. If a life vision is a picture of your ideal future, you can formulate that picture by thinking about the different pieces that fit together to make that picture up.

What does your family life look like in this ideal future? What kind of career do you have? How do you spend your free time? Who are the people around you? All of the different areas of your life that come together to support it and make it a whole are what we can call "pillars." These pillars (or areas) can go by different names, but I find some of the more useful categories to include work, family, romance, health, friendships, finances, contribution, hobbies, home, and spirituality.

Let's drill down a little further. Within each of these life pillars, there are many clues as to what constitutes an ideal life for you. In other words, there are clues as to what would make each area more fulfilling, satisfying, peaceful, exciting, and so on.

These clues are known as *elements*. Elements represent the different criteria that you believe will help you feel satisfied when they are met in a given area of your life. As we gather more and more of these elements for each area, they act as pieces of a puzzle that can be fit together to allow a new life picture to emerge.

In the beginning, it may not be clear whether all of the pieces will actually go well together or even which overall picture you are trying to create. But, from these puzzle pieces or elements, new options and possibilities become apparent. The initial picture of your life vision will be born.

Over time, as you play and experiment, you will be able to select and refine the right vision for you.

Example visions. Let's walk through two examples of individuals on a mission to design their life visions. In the first, you'll see Jill, a late twenty-something who was able to come up with a compelling vision for the career of her dreams after she sat down and conducted the exercise at the start of this chapter. She then took this vision and broke it down into smaller pieces—elements—so she could have the concrete details needed to guide her job search for her ideal career.

In the second example, Tom, a forty-something investment banker, felt more comfortable listing off the elements that he wanted in his family life. He then found that by putting these elements together to describe a bigger-picture vision for his family life, he had a valuable bird's eye map of the life he wanted for himself. He could then use this map at any time to evaluate what was most important to him, where he might want to make changes with his plan, and how true he was staying to his core values.

Let's start with Jill. When she sat down and imagined what her dream life would be like five years from now, this is what she saw.

There she was in Europe, dressed in the latest clothing trends and sitting next to the runway in Milan during Fashion Week, sending her fashion forecasts back to buyers in the States and looking forward to a week's vacation in a villa in Tuscany before she returned to work in New York.

Jill had been asked to design her dream career life, and she came up with nothing less. But now what? How could she take this exciting vision and make it more practical? She and her coach decided to brainstorm about the elements that made up Jill's dream career so she would have a better idea of what she was looking for when job hunting. This led Jill to realize that she ideally wanted a career that included the following:

- ability to follow fashion trends
- opportunities for international travel
- opportunity to use her strengths at analyzing and synthesizing data
- salary of at least 100K
- four weeks of vacation per year.

Jill also realized that a bonus would be if she could occasionally work from home, so she added this item to her list of elements.

With her vision translated into elements, Jill now had a more clear idea of what she was looking for in a job and had latitude to consider all opportunities that matched these elements. She was not married to Milan, for example, but she did want international travel in the fashion industry. And her vacation time and salary had to be enough to allow her to tack on leisure days to her business trips, even if it wasn't always a week's vacation at a given clip.

Now let's take a look at Tom. When asked to build his vision, he chose to start by writing a list of the elements that he wanted to have in his family life. It looked like this:

- go to the gym with my wife every Saturday morning and have lazy Sunday mornings together over the newspaper and coffee
- attend all of my kids' sports events
- go camping for two weeks with the family out West every summer
- Sunday family sit-down dinner each week.

This list represented Tom's dream list of elements for his family life. His wishes were relatively simple, but they captured those things that he longed for and missed as an overworked investment banker. He felt confident that if he could incorporate these elements into his life, he would be much happier.

Next, Tom created a bigger-picture vision that emerged from these elements at the encouragement of his coach, who explained that this would give him more flexibility to determine his real needs and wishes and to redesign his life. When he reflected on the kind of life that his elements were pointing to, Tom developed the following vision:

> In my dream family life, I am an involved dad, and my kids know that I love and support them 100%. We have lots of quality time together and I am able to pass my love of the outdoors on to them. My wife and I have a strong marriage and still enjoy spending time together. Even though I have intense responsibilities at work, I am able to make time for my wife and myself on the weekend so we can relax together and reconnect.

Once Tom had created this vision, he could really see his core values come into play. As he and his coach discussed Tom's wish list of elements, they could tack back to his vision to get ideas for alternate but equally suitable elements when it became clear that Tom was not willing to give up his job as a banker and would not be able to free up the time he needed to gain all of the desired elements.

For example, Tom decided that instead of two weeks of camping out West, he and his family could do a one-week trip every summer and then a few weekend camping trips throughout the rest of the year. He also came to terms with the fact that he wasn't going to be able to make every one of his kids' sporting events but that as long as he could make two games for each of his kids every month, he would feel comfortably involved. And so on.

Sometimes people have a sense of what they want (the vision) but they don't know what the nuts and bolts of that vision might look like (the elements); sometimes people know the pieces (the elements) but not what they add up to (the vision). Whether you start with a vision like Jill or the elements like Tom, you will have the building blocks needed to design the future you're looking to create. Will you be able to attain every element of your vision? Will each element deliver on its promise for happiness? Maybe, maybe not. Those are not the questions we are asking here. Right now, it's simply time to dream. Later, you can make adjustments to change, influence, or accept a situation as needed.

Your turn. For now, let's start with creating a picture of all the good stuff that you want in your life and put it on the canvas so you can eventually take some steps toward creating it. Here are a few more examples to get your thoughts rolling. (When you are ready, you may also want to turn to the *Appendix*, which contains two exercises for creating your life vision.)

In the area of money and finance, do you have a specific number in your head that represents your ideal financial future? Some people

Brainstorm the Elements for Your Life Vision

Take some time now to write down the elements of your life vision. You can focus on one area of your life (such as career or family) or you can choose to take on your life as a whole. Here are some questions that can help you generate elements that you may want to include in your vision. Write down anything that pops into your mind here. It is time to explore!

- What's important to you in your work? Outside of work?
- How about your health and well-being?
- What constitutes a wealthy life for you?
- What is important to you regarding your personal development and growth?
- Who is important to you with regard to your family and your friends?
- What do you want your family and your significant other to be for you in your life?
- Who do you want to be for each of them?
- Describe the ideal physical environment for you. How about where you're working?
- Describe the ideal social and emotional environment for you. How about at work?

- What do you want to do for fun? How do you want to spend your leisure time?
- What is important for you regarding your spiritual and religious beliefs? What role do you want them to play in your future?

From these answers, what larger life picture starts to emerge? Do you see the vision you want to step into, or maybe you need to push past boundaries to create a totally new vision from scratch. Either way, have faith that you can create something for yourself. How could you not when you love all the ingredients?

don't focus on a number but instead have an experiential picture that represents the financial future they seek. For example, their ideal vision in this realm might be the ability to take a vacation when they want or to buy some new clothes without feeling the dread of the credit card bill coming at the end of the month.

When it comes to contribution and service, it's important to some people that they design a life with a component that involves serving other people; for other individuals, this is not as essential. Either way, what's important to note is that there are no should's or judgments here because that doesn't do anyone any good. You are designing the life that *you* want, not the life that someone else feels you should have or that the media, society, or modern culture presents as the perfect or ideal life. Forget the glossy magazines, the shiny car commercials, and the bright lights of the movies for a while and reflect on what *you* want. The goal with these exercises is simply to give yourself the freedom to envision that big, blissful life that can make only *you* happy.

Creating Sacred Space and Time

As you think about crafting your life vision, you are likely to encounter the feeling that you just don't have the time to sit down and do it. Yes, time management is such a huge challenge these days, but creating the time to craft your life vision is *essential*.

Friends, you'll never "find" the time to design your life vision; you have to *create* it. If you are serious about creating your extraordinary life, plan to block out at least thirty interruption-proof minutes to begin. Creating your life vision requires deeper thinking, so anything less than that will not work well.

In fact, you may need to schedule a few of these brainstorming sessions as you get your creative mind back into shape and as the picture of your desired future unfolds. Additionally, try to use sensory aids to create the mood and energy that will carry you into this creative state of mind. For me, it's unplugging all of my digital appendages (e.g., my cell phone and PDA), putting on some mellow music (I prefer acoustic guitar or piano), and going into our four-season sun room, which has big windows on three sides and looks out over our property.

I can't emphasize how important it is to get away from the daily noise. Deepak Chopra explains this by stating that no one will hear it when the biggest skyscraper is thrown into a turbulent sea. But even the smallest pebble makes a big ripple in a calm lake.[4] The constant, daily noise in our lives prevents our deeper thoughts from emerging and being heard. This is partially why we stay in reactive mode most of the time—who has time to think these days?

If I hadn't gotten away from my office to have lunch on September 10th, I don't think I would have had the mental space to reflect on my life and ultimately come up with the simple idea of having breakfast with my family. In many ways, deciding to create quiet space to reflect on things that day is what saved my life.

Now, it's your turn. Your peace of mind and happiness are worth it. Aren't they?

Focus on What, Not How

As you go through the exercise of defining your elements and crafting your vision, don't get stuck trying to figure out how you're going to make it happen. There will be plenty of time for practicalities—for considerations, qualifications, accommodations, and adaptations. But we are not there yet. Right now, we are trying to paint a picture of what an ideal future looks like for you; we are focusing on *what*, not *how*.

As a result, don't worry if the elements, dreams, or pictures you're painting as you create your vision seem unrealistic or unattainable. Know that *there is always a way.* Always!

Turning a 4-Hour Commute Into 24 Minutes

When I knew that I wanted to change careers to have my own coaching business, I was aware that it might take some time to make the transition. So while I maintained my corporate job and continually tried to make the most of that experience, I also explored opportunities to somehow reduce my two-hour-each-way, four-hour daily commute. At first, I had no idea what to do, so I looked for the smallest step I could take to get started.

After some research and outreach, I learned that there was a satellite office that was a twelve-minute drive from my home. Now that was a commute I could deal with! The challenge was that it was a local sales office and I was in a national corporate role. In other words, I was not a revenue-producer but rather attached to a cost center. My salary and expenses were covered in the corporate budget, but if I moved to that sales office, it would be a direct cost to their bottom line. Not quite an enticing proposition for an office that was measured by its profitability.

In fact, everyone I spoke to told me that there was no way someone with my corporate role could be based out of a local sales office. It had never been done and couldn't be done. But you know my mantra: there's always a way. If I can't, then I must.

I started by finding a viable business reason for me to visit the office. At the time, I was in charge of a training team that spanned the country. I had also built an internal network of managers that represented every single office in the United States. Therefore, it wasn't hard to come up with a training program that I could personally deliver to the key sales people in that local office.

Little by little, I led more training programs there, developed a relationship with the head of the office, and started working from there one day a week, which became two days per week, which ultimately had me relocating my office to the local sales office. It took eighteen months for all of that to happen. All of the little steps I was taking would ultimately add up to something that made a huge difference in my life. People told me it couldn't be done, but with the right plan and perseverance, it could!

So even if you don't know right now how you're going to get to your vision in the future, I want you to trust that you will find a way later. We'll worry about how to make it happen in the *Planning* section.

I know that the doubts and worry are not easy to set aside. At this point in the process, many people actually hit a wall and begin to make assumptions. They hear themselves saying, "I can't," "It's not realistic," or "It's just not possible!" The problem is that you are defining what's "possible" based on very limited knowledge of what *is* actually possible. Here are some common beliefs that might get in your way. We will explore them so you can recognize them and then work through them.

"I can't do that." Don't judge yourself! We are so good at that! A thought comes to mind and before we even write it down, the judge inside of us says something like, "That's stupid," "I can't do that," "I don't know what I want to do," or "I'm not good at anything."

The judge inside us is very clever, and because it sounds like it knows what it's talking about, we listen! And we've been listening to it for a long time! Do your best to suspend your inner judge—give him or her a short vacation so you can explore these ideas and questions fully.

"You can't do that." I'm sure you've heard the expression, "Too many cooks spoil the broth." No matter how you begin to define your vision and its elements, expect people to say things like, "You can't do that." However, it's important to remember that these people are coming from their own perspectives of what's possible. They have their own risk tolerances, limiting beliefs, preferences, and elements that are unique and different from yours. What may be their truth is not necessarily your truth. Don't let other people's views stop you in this early stage of the process.

"That's impossible." Too many times we (falsely) see things as not possible or feasible, and we just say, "That's not possible." Just because it doesn't exist for you, doesn't mean it doesn't exist! There are many, many worlds out there awaiting your discovery. Life is a process that unfolds each moment. Remember, everything you enjoy today was at some point out of your perceived reach. Doors that you didn't even know existed will open for you tomorrow.

Think about the Internet, television, the airplane, the automobile, and the light bulb! What if the inventors of these amazing machines and devices had stopped at "It's not possible"?! Instead of saying, "It's impossible," how about trying, "I don't know if it's possible." In that small rephrasing, you open yourself up to the possibility that it can exist, as in "I don't know, but I'm willing to find out."

I once had a client who shared with me how much he loved playing guitar (element). He said jokingly during one of our sessions, "Wouldn't it be great if someone would pay me to play guitar all day?" (vision). Aside from being in a famous band, who gets paid for playing music all day? Sounds impossible, right? Well, after some research and exploration, my client discovered that there are actually guitar-manufacturing companies out there that pay people to test their guitars before they go to market. And guess what? Eventually, my client became one of them. It's true. After wishing he could make a living playing guitar all day, he landed a job doing just that.

He wasn't the only one who managed to fulfill a "crazy" vision. I had another client who worked for a nonprofit agency and dreamed of singing and dancing in her own one-woman show. One year later, I was sitting in the audience at the New York Fringe Festival, watching her perform the show that she wrote, directed, produced, and starred in by herself. And, yes, there was also singing and dancing. You see, anything is possible. Don't let your assumptions stop you from dreaming because your assumptions are based on beliefs that may not be true.

Many people ask me how I made the jump from Corporate Marketer to The Human WakeUp Call. After 9/11, I knew I wanted to make a career change, but I had no vision of what kind of work I was looking for. What I did know was that I loved working with people—training and teaching them. But I was very much in the "I can't make a living doing that" corner.

And then one day, six little words gave me the catalyst I was looking for.

One weekend at home, we were in the kitchen and my wife's friend Jen casually turned to me and said, "You would make a great coach." Initially, that meant nothing to me. I said, "Sure, when Olivia is older I'd love to coach her in soccer." She said, "No, I mean you would make a great *life* coach."

I asked her, "What the heck is a life coach?" I had never heard of that phrase before, though it did sound intriguing. She went on to tell me that it was something she had recently learned about, and when she had heard of it, she immediately thought of me.

On any other day, I would have likely thanked her for the suggestion and then let the thought slip past like so many hidden treasures that go unrecognized. But that day I immediately started my research. The more I looked into it, the more excited I became. For the first time, I felt pulled toward a world I was compelled to be a part of.

Those six little words had unlocked a world of new possibilities, a world that five minutes earlier didn't exist for me. Yet, it had been there the whole time. My entire life shifted from that one statement, and I have never looked back.

I tell this story now as if it was a magical moment where the clouds parted and the sun shone through—and in a way it was—but I also want you to see that the day Jen stood in my kitchen was just an ordinary day like any other. But it was an ordinary day filled *with possibility*. Every day has that possibility inherent in it. What made this day different was my *openness* to that possibility.

You too are surrounded by possibility. But you can only uncover that possibility if you are willing to start by asking *what* and save *how* for later. When you start to ask what, the signs and clues will present themselves to you *and*, most importantly, you will notice them! You will have the raw material you need to begin formulating your vision.

Conclusion

When it comes to your vision, you can start wherever you are and then build on it over time. For example, you can focus on one area of your life for starters—work or family. Or maybe you'd just like to focus on a vision for the short or medium-term—what you want your life to look like a few months or a year from now. If it helps, start small. The point is that visions don't have to be these intimidating life projects you'll never complete. They can be small and then grow organically over time.

But that word *time* is key. You must *make* time in order to create your vision. So make time to dream. Give yourself permission to imagine your perfect life five years from now and then consider all the elements that will help you get to that future life. That life is out there waiting for you. I promise.

Now promise me that you won't get stuck trying to figure out how you're going to make it happen or whether it's even possible in the first place. That's focusing on *what*, not *how*. Even if the elements, dreams, or pictures you're painting as you create your vision seem unrealistic or unattainable, just remember *there is always a way.*

In the end, your life won't look exactly like your vision. It can't possibly. There are too many unknowns and too many variables. That's not the point. You are becoming aware of the things that are most important to you—the elements that you want to have as part of your life. As you continue to explore, discover, and define them, you will have a greater ability to integrate them into your life.

Have fun uncovering and discovering your new life. It's out there waiting for you . . .

PLAY

"To know without doing is not to know."
~Fern Gorin, Founder and Director of the Life Purpose Institute

9

Climb Into the Sandbox

"We think too small, like the frog at the bottom of the well. He thinks the sky is only as big as the top of the well. If he surfaced, he would have an entirely different view."

~Mao Tse-Tung

My son Sam is a funny kid. His nickname is "Moosher" because he's such a mush. He loves to hug and is always very affectionate. You know where you stand with him at any given moment. The challenge is that at eight years old, he's ninety-four pounds and four feet, nine inches tall (!) But he loves to play, and he loves to try new things. I'll be outside grilling (one of my favorite things to do), and he'll say, "Dad, can I try?" I'll be putting together a new pitchback or soccer net, and when I ask him if he wants to help, his typical response is "sure." He's up for anything. No qualms about it.

On a recent trip to Disney, Sam wanted to ride every single ride in the park, no matter how big. He had no fear. As I was watching him, I thought, "Wow. What a sense of freedom. He has no hesitation to simply play and learn along the way." If only we adults could keep that fearlessness and hunger alive for playing and discovering new things, we could have so many more great experiences. Kids have none of the junk that adults start creating for themselves when trying to preserve their image or save face. Nope. If we were more like them, we could just play, get our hands dirty, get ketchup on our shirts, learn, fall down, get up, and try it again.

This section is one of the most important ones in this book because it's here that we take the concepts you developed earlier and turn them into experience, what I call "principles into action." It's here that your ideas, dreams, and concepts are brought to life and that you get to wear a crazed face like Dr. Frankenstein (it's pronounced *Frunkensteen*) and scream, "It's alive!"

In this chapter, we'll begin by exploring what I mean by "playing" within the present framework and uncover a few reasons why it is so important to play when it comes to making significant life changes. We'll also talk about how playing bigger in your life is not just an action but a mindset.

Up until now, we've investigated many ideas and concepts, but now is the time to *get in action* on this journey. You will get many benefits from simply reading this book, but the magic—the real transformation of your life—will occur only through your actions. In other words, it's time for you to move from watching the game on the couch, to playing the game on the field. This is the moment of truth—when you get on that path and take those first newborn steps toward your new reality. You may wobble or you may fall. Is that okay? You bet. You're learning to walk!

What Is Playing?

Take a moment now to think about your vision for your life, and grab a hold of one of the pieces that might seem really far away, daunting, or even scary. For me, it was the part of my vision that had me working for myself, no longer tied to a secure, corporate organization that could provide health insurance, retirement benefits, or a good salary. For you, it might be something else.

Playing is the secret to managing that fear and hedging against the risks of moving into doing something new. Instead of my having to quit my corporate job right at the start and lose all that security before I even knew for sure that coaching was for me, I started by *playing* as a coach. This involved me talking to other coaches, taking coaching classes, and then coaching my first clients at night and on weekends while keeping my day job. Before I made a dramatic switch in my life to a totally new profession and new way of supporting myself and my family, I could just play and see if I really wanted to be a coach after all.

Playing is all about trying something new in order to gain experience and understanding without having to fully commit to any change just yet. In the process of simply playing, you'll expand your boundaries of what you believe to be possible as you break through the blocks and hang-ups that might have stopped you before. To unlock your potential and move away from "fine," you will need to experience and face these fears and blocks. Academics and theories won't get you there. Experience will.

The first time people hear me say "play," they tend to think of a connection to the way that children play, and there is some truth to that connection. It's called "play" because you want to bring that same sense of openness, wonder, and learning to this experience as you did when you were a child. As you play and test out new areas of life, this open mindset will give you the best sense of what it's truly like to be in that new life—as well as give you the courage to try it in the first place. But playing is more than just kid stuff.

Using a sports analogy, think of playing like spring training or preseason football. You're practicing your new pitches, experimenting with different strategies, and even trying out new positions. However, regardless of whether you score more runs/points/goals than your opponent, the games don't count. You're there to increase your conditioning, get your muscles stronger, and adjust to the speed of the game—basically, to get into game shape. That's what playing is like. It's going to get you into game shape for later when it's time for the season to begin and the games to count.

In developing a further understanding of this concept, let's take a look at the *opposite* of playing. Think of not playing as simply being a spectator in the cheap seats, just watching the game. You'll have plenty of commentary on what the players should or should not be doing—maybe even applauding or booing their moves, yet you are still the observer. From that vantage point, everyone's an expert and thinks they know how the game should be played. But as we shared in the quote that began this section, "to know without doing is not to know." Playing requires you to leave your comfortable seat and get yourself onto that field. It is unquestionably more challenging to be a player than a fan, but it's also more exciting and rewarding. Let's look at some of the benefits that you'll enjoy when becoming more engaged in your own game.

Why Play?

Play is one of the richest tools out there when it comes to creating your ideal life. As you engage more fully and stretch your own boundaries, you will experience many benefits that will positively impact your life. You get to try something out before you fully commit to it. Play helps us learn new things and work through any fears that have prevented us from moving forward in the past, including that all-powerful fear of the unknown. Playing also opens up entire new worlds of possibility that we never knew existed, which will lead to brand new opportunities and levels of success. Let's take a closer look at each of these.

Taste before you buy. Before you rearrange your life and jump into the deep end to pursue your new vision, you want to make sure that you're committing to something that you truly want. By playing, you get to dip your toe into the pool and experience firsthand what those changes might feel like, before having to take the plunge. If you discover during the play stage that you don't care for something nearly as much as you thought you would, you have not risked much of anything. You can simply fine tune or even completely change your direction and then play some more until you are confident you're pursuing the right path.

Just like when you go to an ice cream parlor and see a new flavor. Triple ripple peanut butter fudge may sound good, but are you going to buy an ice cream cake with that flavor for your child's birthday and risk that it tastes lousy? Some of you might, but most of you won't—it all depends on your tolerance for risk. Instead, you're likely to ask for a taste to see if you like it first. The point is that you want to taste it before you buy it.

Here's an example of what I mean. Let's say that you've always wanted to own a health club. Health and fitness have always been important to you. Looking at some of the elements of this vision, you love to exercise, you are conscious about the relationship between nutrition and energy, and you often find yourself willingly assisting others and sharing your knowledge with them. You dream about the flexibility and independence that owning your own business will provide for you.

Before you borrow money from your Uncle Al and invest all the time and resources into opening the club, though, you can first play in that world of health clubs: talk to other owners and managers, take a course on club management, work at one on weekends, and visit a number of different clubs to note what they're doing and how they're doing it. Playing will allow you to go behind the magic curtain to see if health club ownership really provides you with what you hoped and expected. What is it really like to be the owner of a club (not just what you think it's like)? What is the lifestyle like? What are you not seeing?

What else can you learn? Who else can you meet to support you and what kind of experience can you add to your arsenal for when it's time to jump in?

That's why it is so important to define those elements that are core to you (as you did in the *Purpose* section). They are crucial factors in determining what avenue you hope to pursue. But an understanding of your values alone won't get you there. Now it's time to experience what your "ideal" life might be like so you can see—and feel—if you really want to go for it. As a result of your play-filled experience, you may end up completely changing your life vision . . . or you may become even hungrier for it! Whatever your new pursuit may be, playing in that world before jumping into the deep end helps you make sure there's water in the pool.

Face fears, learn new things, and build confidence. Although I hope that playing is fun for you, the kind of play that I am talking about here is not only about having fun (as I mentioned a little bit earlier). In fact, sometimes you might be downright terrified to play. It's a natural tendency for people to stay in a place where they feel comfortable, safe, and secure. That's where "fine" lives. It is only when you travel outside of your comfort zone, and you face your fears, that you learn new things and build confidence. You've already begun to do this when you allowed yourself to dream and create a vision for yourself. Playing will now push you toward new behaviors and out of your complacency so that you can discover that you can do it . . . if you want it badly enough.

My client Rich had done some research on a new industry, sports marketing, that he hoped to move into. One of the first things we agreed he could do to explore that industry further was to speak with people who were already employed successfully there. This is a form of play. His assignment was to conduct informational interviews with five people in sports marketing to learn about what it really looked like from the inside. However, he found out very quickly how uncomfortable he was reaching out to people he didn't know. He was a manager in his current position and had no difficulty in managing his team, speaking with customers, and completing his daily responsibilities. But for some reason, when it came to making a cold call to a stranger, asking for help for himself, he became paralyzed.

As his coach, I used the old adage of, "If you can't do it, then you must do it" and reduced the assignment from contacting five people to just making a single phone call. We role-played and explored as many possible outcomes as we could think of to build his confidence and courage. Then, we reinforced the notion that he was simply exploring new worlds; he was not giving up his stable job or engaging in any behaviors that were reckless or dangerous. He was just making a phone call to learn more about this other world. By emphasizing that he was merely playing, it took enough pressure off of him that he was able to make a real commitment to the task.

Guess what? Rich called me a few days later and told me that he faced his fear about calling people and had spent *two hours* on the phone speaking to this one contact. The contact was even going to introduce him to three other people who worked in sports marketing. "Now I want to make twenty phone calls!" Rich said. This was a huge step out of his comfort zone, but he learned a lot from his experience. He moved forward with his networking and eventually got a job in this new field . . . all because he summoned up the courage to get out of his comfort zone and play.

Like Rich, playing enables us to make new friends, learn about our areas of interest, and develop a support network that will teach us how the new game is actually played!

Discover new worlds of possibility. Let's return to our earlier example of owning a health club. As a result of your spending a few days shadowing a health club owner, you realized that the reality of owning your own health club didn't support your desire for flexibility and independence. In fact, it was quite the opposite—continual long hours and constant pressure. That was an important lesson to learn and was a direct result of you playing first.

Additionally, while shadowing the owner, you discovered another interest—a love for creating experiences for others. After speaking with the owner, you found out that he hired a company to consult him on designing everything in the club from the traffic flow to the way the smoothie bar was setup, to the layout and lighting of the entire space. In your research of this consulting firm, you discovered that there is an entire industry devoted to health club consulting that helps owners create the kind of ambiance and customer experience they are seeking.

Had you not played and visited the health club owner, you wouldn't have realized that this other world of club consulting even existed. As a result of playing, you now have more clarity about what you don't want as well as an entirely new option to explore.

There's a great website run by my colleague Brian Kurth called Vocation Vacations where you can spend a weekend as an apprentice for hundreds of different occupations.[5] Some are as basic as a Bed and Breakfast Owner, but there are more exotic ones as well, such as Raising Alpacas, Oyster Farming, Sports Radio Announcing, being a Brew Master for a beer company, and being a Sword Maker (yes, real swords), to name just a few. See what I mean? There are truly entire *worlds* of possibility out there that you don't even know exist. And you have the freedom—through play—to check them out.

By playing, you'll discover these new worlds as well as develop a much deeper understanding of your own preferences, style, and desires, all of which can feed back into a new version of your vision, one based on knowing through experience.

Now that you have a sense of what play is, let's shake things up and push you further to not just try to play, but to play big. I want you to be able to get not just the meat and the potatoes, but the gravy, the cranberry sauce, and the apple pie *with* the ice cream.

What am I talking about when I say playing big? Well, that's going to depend on who you are, what you want from your life, and where the boundaries of your comfort zone lie. When I encourage you to play big, I'm talking about allowing yourself to transform the *anything is possible* philosophy into *I can do anything*. It's time to transfer that open-minded perspective into hands-on playing. Playing big means going outside of your comfort zone in order to learn more, create a healthy support network, and gain all the experience and knowledge you need to transition into your new, ideal life.

This is not a one-time deal. In fact, I believe that playing big is a powerful mindset. It's not a destination but rather a whole approach to living. Growth is continual and so is playing big. Each time you catch your breath and start getting comfortable, it's time to start thinking about playing bigger. Remember, we need to continuously confuse our muscles to keep them growing. By continuing to seek ways to play big, you will be constantly flexing and exercising your own "play-big" muscles. This will provide benefits such as incredible personal power, a sense of accomplishment, more adventure, and more ease, as well as leading you in the discovery of new worlds. Little things that used to stop you before will now seem doable. As these muscles continue to grow strong, what was playing big last time is now no big deal.

Let me give you some examples.

My client, Susan, had a vision to write and perform in a one-woman show in a small club in Greenwich Village in New York City (I mentioned her earlier). Yet she started "small" with singing lessons. As Susan developed, she kept playing even bigger, eventually performing her own show—not in a small club, but live on stage for two straight weeks at the New York Fringe Festival. Reading up on the coaching profession on my computer was playing "small"; speaking in front of hundreds of people at the Network for Executive Women Leadership Summit was playing big.

It doesn't always have to be as big as those examples. Take someone who is afraid of public speaking—always at the top of the list in terms of "Things People Dislike." For him or her, standing up during a lecture and asking the speaker a question might be completely nerve-racking. As we discussed earlier, for my client Rich, simply making a phone call to a stranger to do an informational interview conjured up real fear. But look at how there's always some kind of breakthrough on the other side—some level of freedom and confidence to be gained by stretching beyond those boundaries. That one phone call literally changed his life.

The challenge is that playing bigger is not the easier road; it's the harder road. It's much easier and much safer to keep floating down the river than to play bigger. Gravity, inertia, and complacency can make it seem impossible to play big. Our fears and worries, and all those critical voices inside of us are trying to stop us in order to "protect" us and keep us safe. They say, "Stay where you are. Don't make any changes; things are fine exactly the way they are. Don't even think about doing that. Are you crazy? It's selfish to risk what you already have. Why would you even consider that? It's dangerous out there."

But think of the cost of doing nothing—of not playing big. If you reflect back over the course of your life, I bet you can find at least ten instances where you played bigger in some way and it fundamentally changed the course of your life. You took that new job, moved to a new home, got married, had a child (or four), raised your hand and took on that project, whatever. These big activities all shifted the trajectory your life was on. What if you hadn't done any of those things? Remember, we are not here to make things *fine*. We are here to create a life that's much bigger and better than fine.

Back when I was working in the World Trade Center, I had a colleague, Rob, who always talked about how much he wanted to create and run a sports league—activities such as co-ed softball, volleyball, etc. There were a number of leagues that already existed in NYC at the time, and I thought it would be pretty hard to create a new sports league in the city.

But Rob was undeterred—he kept talking about how one day he'd like to run a great league that also donated part of the proceeds to charity. Like me, he was not at his desk on 9/11 and was therefore spared on that day.

Spurred by his gift of another day, Rob Herzog went on to found ZogSports, a co-ed social sports league for young professionals with a charity focus.[6] His company organizes recreational sports leagues and donates 10% of profit to charity. Rob's company is now in the New York metro area; Washington, DC; and Hartford, CT and is expanding to other locations soon. ZogSports has about 80,000 people participating in their activities and has donated over $1.2 million to charity. That's playing big!

There's a great quote by Marianne Williamson that's been cited many times, and I want to share part of it now because it reminds us that we have an obligation to play bigger.

> Our deepest fear is not that we're inadequate, our deepest fear is that we're powerful beyond measure, it's our light not our darkness that most frightens us. We ask ourselves who am I to be brilliant, gorgeous, talented, and fabulous? Well actually who are you not to be? . . . Your playing small doesn't serve the world. There's nothing enlightened about shrinking so that other people won't feel insecure around you . . . . As we let our own light shine we unconsciously give other people permission to do the same.

As Williamson says, we're not supposed to suppress ourselves because we're afraid it's going to make other people feel uncomfortable. We must live up to our own potential so we can give other people permission to do the same thing! When they see us playing big, they may feel inspired to do the same. Imagine a world where we all played bigger. What affect would that have on the global economy? The environment? Impoverished children around the world?

Regardless of its form, playing big is about getting out of your comfort zone and going for something that has the potential to make a positive difference in your own or others' lives. So the question really is—what does playing big look like for you? It's time to consider the possibilities.

Conclusion

It's one thing to think and design changes that you want to make for your life, and it's quite another to actually take an action step toward one of them. This is not the easier road; it's the harder road. It's much more comfortable and much "safer" to keep floating down the river. Sure, there are many reasons (ahem, "excuses") that we come up with to validate why we should stay exactly where we are.

"Things are fine."

"Why rock the boat?"

"Why screw up what I have?"

However, we've already established that you are here because you want more—more success, more happiness, more adventure, more meaning, more whatever. Now's your chance to play bigger.

This is where most of us fall down. That's why we introduce the concept of playing—to lessen some of the stress, fear, and discomfort that might otherwise hold you back from even trying.

Now it's time to create an experience for yourself to expand your current boundaries of what you believe in all of your heart and head to be possible. Where those boundaries are planted in the ground is where your current limits of what's possible exist. Your mind can only take you a certain distance. People in Berlin needed to believe that one day the wall could come down, but it wasn't going to actually crumble until action was taken. We need to start chipping away at your wall so you can see the limitless fields of possibility that lie beyond it, just like the frog in the well.

Just play.

10

Let the Games Begin

"Twenty years from now you will be more disappointed by the things you didn't do than by the ones you did. So throw off the bowlines. Sail away from the safe harbor. Catch the trade winds in your sails. Explore. Dream."

~Mark Twain

Okay, so we've just done a lot of brain work on the concept of play—what is it? What can it look like? What does it mean to play bigger? This chapter is going to give you two of my favorite techniques for getting comfortable actually playing.

Play is really about taking an approach of ready, fire, aim (rather than ready, aim, fire). Firing without aiming? Playing without a full-scale plan? Doing something without already being perfect? For most of us, that's not an easy concept.

Don't worry, you may feel unsure or even totally clueless as to how you're going to get from Point A to Points B, C, and D, but take courage in the fact that everything you need is there waiting for you to discover it. But it can't be discovered if you are just sitting on your butt. Think about it. Christopher Columbus may have been looking for a new trade route to Asia when he set out in 1492, but he discovered something far more important. America was waiting for Columbus to "discover" it—yet it was already out there and had been inhabited for thousands of years! However, he had to get on the ship and start exploring. This is where play comes in . . . you have to get into action to discover everything that's out there waiting for you.

As you will see later in this chapter, you also need to be willing to give up a little control in order to start playing. Imagine a little kid in a game of make-believe. Does she play the part of the horse by quietly standing in one place saying "nay," or does she gallop all around the room, yelling "Nay-Nay-Nay" at the top of her lungs till her voice gets scratchy? If we take our cues from kids, we will see that we have to let go of some of our inhibitions in order to really play.

So much learning happens when we play. In this chapter, I will try to take you on that journey so you are able to really play in a way that will get you closer to that ideal life you've started to design for yourself. Let the games begin . . .

Where Do You Begin?

Okay, so you are ready to start playing now that you've defined your purpose, but you find yourself hesitating, not knowing what to do next, or feeling scared. Guess what? You don't have to have all the answers yet, and it's okay to be nervous. You don't even have to have a plan (ready, fire, aim, remember?) Playing is about getting out there and just doing it. Let's look at an example.

What would happen if one day you decided you wanted to hold a fundraising event for charity even though you'd never done it before? You had no plan, no past experience, and no answers—just enthusiasm and a few ideas. What would happen if you just decided to play—to go for it and see what you could come up with? Would you be able to raise any money? Would you be able to create an event to remember?

Several years ago, I started with a very simple but vague idea—I wanted to create an event that would involve my friends, that would involve an artistic endeavor, and that would be good for charity. It also had to be something I could do outside of my full-time job. But what would it be? I couldn't really figure it out until I started to play—which at first was talking to people. I simply shared the idea I had with everyone I could think of and before I knew it, the experience started to come together.

"Why don't you use my lounge and I'll just donate it to you?" the local cigar seller said to me. I hadn't even known he had a downstairs lounge until I started talking to him. "What can we sell?" I wondered out loud to friends. Someone said, "Why not have an amateur photography show?" And so on until the whole event—once a vague idea—became a very rewarding reality.

The night of the event, we turned the cigar lounge into an art gallery, with 8X10 or larger photos submitted from my friends and family—their best shots. We auctioned the photos, along with other goods and items I had gotten donated by walking door to door around the neighborhood and asking for contributions. In the process, my friends and I had a fantastic time and we made $1,000 for charity!

You see, that whole experience was just waiting for me to create it; it just needed someone to bring it to life. I had an idea and I played with it and I tried to make it bigger and bigger and that's how I got from Point A to Point D.

When I started to play, I had no idea how much I would learn and how many times the "universe" would pop up with new ideas to help the project take on a life of its own. All because I was willing to get out there and play.

Here's an interesting idea. What if everything already existed, but it was just waiting for you to bring it to your life? I call this concept "It's All Already Ready" (say that 428 times fast). Think of the best party you ever hosted, or the best performance—athletic or dramatic—you ever gave. Before you ran a six-minute mile, you didn't know whether it could happen. Before you had the party, you wondered how good it would actually be. Then, it happened, and it became part of reality. Looking back, it seems as though these realities already existed. You just had to make them happen.

What is out there waiting for you to discover and create? Do you have an idea but are not sure how to push it to the next level? Remind yourself that it is all do-able—because it is, in fact, already out there. You just have to start somewhere.

If you talked to one hundred people about the work you do, might something be created by that? When I work with independent sales reps, to open up hidden streams of opportunities, I encourage them to perform the following exercise, just to play and see what is created as a result. I have them walk into every store on Main Street and introduce themselves to the proprietors, sharing what they do for a living. Not selling, not seeking referrals, not asking for anything. Simply making an introduction and building rapport. One client developed a great referral source for his financial planning practice; another learned about the local Chamber of Commerce, which she then joined and had a new network to connect with. One even met that "someone special" who was shopping in the store and overheard his conversation. Sometimes nothing comes out of it right away.

The point is that you don't know what can be created until you get out there and play. It's all waiting for you; you just haven't done it yet.

Become a Dancing Fool

When I "played" with creating my charity fundraiser, I managed to motivate several other people to play alongside me. But sometimes others are the ones who have motivated me to play and let go.

Let me tell you a story about just that . . .

As a coach, I need to keep my own coaching skills and practices sharp. So I decided it was time for me to go see the "master" and attend my first Tony Robbins seminar. For those who don't know who he is, Tony is one of the world's top motivational speakers and leaders of personal and professional change.

I had never been to one of Robbins' seminars before and had mixed feelings about him leading up to that point. I had heard some great things about his events, but I needed to experience it for myself, make my own judgments and define my own opinions. I needed to determine whether he was as authentic as he seemed or whether he was all smoke and mirrors.

After all, I was "in the business" and prided myself on my own authenticity and the level of genuineness I bring to my work, so I would surely know if Robbins was peddling snake oil or if he truly walked his talk. At first, I thought I'd go into the seminar as an observer, trying to learn as much as I could about how to create a successful, large-scale event. (Modeling others who are doing what you are doing at a higher level is a great way to learn and grow without having to reinvent the wheel.) But I also wanted to be a participant and really experience the program from my seat to see how Robbins' magic worked on me, if at all.

In order to do this fully, it meant I would have to really play—get out of my thinking head and let go of believing that I already "knew" everything, since I had a lot of experience speaking in front of a live audience. We tend to "already know" when we're faced with doing something that we have experience with. However, that's really just a beautiful excuse not to engage or play and we're cheating ourselves out of a new experience.

Another barrier for me was that I also had to stop worrying about looking bad, even when we were asked to do something that seemed silly or stupid. That was going to be more challenging as my "I'm not interested" excuse was screaming full tilt within me. Personally, I was never the silly type, dancing and bouncing around, following the crowd, or doing something because everyone around me was doing it. No, I usually kept my thick cloak of judgment wrapped around me, keeping me safe and stopping me from looking foolish.

So for this event I had a decision to make. Was I going to remain an observer, which was much more comfortable? Or was I going to play full out and be a student, participating completely, getting outside of my comfort zone, and letting go of all of my judgments and reservations as they came?

I challenged myself to be a student and promised that I would continually let go of my resistance and go with the flow, following *every instruction* of Robbins' to really understand and experience the potential impact of his program.

So there I was, the first morning of the program, amidst the army of enthusiastic volunteers and followers who were high-fiving everyone who passed. I could feel my judgment setting in immediately—"Are you kidding me? Can you really be that excited this early in the morning? What are you trying to sell me? You're being too happy, dude—tone it down." Many of these folks had a knowing look as they made direct eye contact with us newcomers, as if to say, "I know what you're about to experience and I'll see you on the other side."

I found that experience disconcerting because I was normally the one giving that same look to students and participants at *my* engagements. I wasn't used to being on the receiving end of it. Still, I remembered my promise to myself to be fully present and engaged, and I begrudgingly let go of my judgment.

If you've ever been to a Tony Robbins event, you know he has you standing and jumping up and down for most of the duration. That was hard for me. I was never a comfortable dancer (without a few drinks in me at least, but then watch out!), always pretty reserved and controlled physically. But he was bouncing up and down as were most people around me, raising their hands to the sky.

Though I intended to be a participant, I couldn't help judging these "followers" for doing this ridiculous stuff. I was also looking around the room for other "non-jumpers" to give me some comfort in my decision to not be a blind loyalist. I spotted Nick, and we shared that cynical eye roll and the knowing nod that said, "This is stupid and I'm not doing this crap." I found comfort in our small community of two, empowering the part of me that "wasn't interested" while my promise to be a student waned.

At that moment, I realized how pervasive my need for being in control was. As I looked around at the joyful expressions of the "jumpers," it became clear that while it may have felt like I was benefitting from staying safe, in control, and not looking bad, I was missing out on the chance to generate joy, energy, and pure fun. With this realization, I allowed myself to play—a small jump here, a smile there, and some quick dancing in between. I started letting go. The result? By the end of the day, I was dancing, bouncing, and high fiving.

Did I feel silly and even somewhat stupid? Absolutely! That didn't just go away. But I had developed a new ease and freedom that I hadn't realized I craved so much. It felt great letting go as I got past the initial discomfort. I realized how locked up I was and how it affected so many areas of my life, preventing me from being more playful with my wife, my kids, and just in general! Then I looked across the room at Nick. He was a dancing fool too.

Letting Go to Play

Where are you locked up? What are the boundaries you are defining for yourself? Where are you stopping yourself because of the need to look good or stay in control? What if you were to let go? What would happen? What if the fears or discomfort didn't hold you back anymore? What would that provide for you? What freedom or ease might be created?

You may feel stupid or uncomfortable, and you may look around for partners in crime that give you the perfect excuse to stay exactly where you are in your comfort zone. I say, let go. Play full out despite your doubts and discomfort. Give it a chance—the magic happens over time. You need to cross that bridge and get to the other side where freedom and ease are waiting for you.

Why do you need that freedom and ease? That's a nice state of mind to be in, but it's more than that. Freedom and ease will give you the courage to push yourself even further out of your comfort zone until you ultimately get from today to the tomorrow you've rewritten for yourself.

In what areas could you grow if you allowed yourself to let go and play not just a little, but a lot? Where in your life would you like to become a dancing fool?

How to Play

So now you know "it's" already out there waiting for you and it's up to you to overcome those inhibitions and take a first step. What can you do? Start small. In the case of my charity event, I started with an idea that wasn't even fully developed yet. But as I took those small steps to start playing, I learned that I didn't have to know everything ahead of time, I just had to engage other people in helping me bring the idea to life. Similarly, you don't need to have all the answers at the start. You just need to be willing to start playing. Talk to someone you know. Get on the Internet. Go for a run and open your mind up to that question of what to do next. Take a class or write in your journal. Take one small step and see where it takes you.

Here are some ideas from the Life Purpose Institute for what you can do to research, learn, and test out an idea, and play. While these lean toward career design and exploration, derivations of them can be applied to almost any change you are considering:

- go to organizational meetings
- use an online network (e.g., LinkedIn) or ask friends for contacts to set up informational interviews
- attend industry trade shows and conventions
- go to the library and ask the reference librarian to help you (p.s. libraries have become tremendous resources)
- volunteer or work part-time in your field of interest or work in a related area where you can learn/explore some skills
- go back to school and do research on your field or take a class (or classes) related to the field of interest
- find a mentor in the business and shadow or apprentice with them
- read blogs, magazines, and newsletters related to that field

- follow leaders from that field (e.g., "Follow" them on Twitter, become a Fan of theirs on Facebook)*
- go to S.C.O.R.E. (through U.S. Small Business Administration) or Small Business Development Center (usually through Chamber of Commerce) for free business assistance
- talk to a magazine editor of trade publications (online versions as well)
- talk to professors at a local university or college
- go to stores that carry products related to your field
- hire a consultant or someone with the knowledge you need
- share your idea with others.**

You may be wondering how each or any of these single steps will lead you to the ideal life you pictured for yourself in the previous section of the book. How exactly does Door A (in front of you today) really lead to Door D (waiting for you somewhere in your ideal future)?

Let's put it this way. You're trying to get from where you are to where you want to be. You're not sure how to get there and that's okay. In fact, it's quite normal. This shows up in thoughts such as "I can't make a living doing that!" or "I'm too old to start down that path" or even simply "I don't know how." Because the path is not clear, you may presume it's not possible.

Well, unless you can call Scottie to "beam you up" to the place you want to be, it's going to take more than one step to get there. You first need to walk through Door A—that is the first playing you'll do. Once you have entered the World of A, your experience there will reveal new possibilities for you to try, some of which you didn't even know existed!

---

*   By the way, I would love for you to follow me on Twitter (@HumanWakeUpCall) and on Facebook (Mike Jaffe–Human WakeUp Call).

**   Copyright Fern Gorin and the Life Purpose Institute (www.LifePurposeInstitute.com). Used with permission.

This is where new possibilities emerge—by stepping through that first door and exploring that initial world.

Pretty soon, by playing some more, you have an idea of how to get to Door B. Now, there's a new set of actions to take and a new threshold to cross to step into this new world where new possibilities await you. This continues until you can see Door D ahead of you, and for the first time you see how it might be possible that you can get from A to D. But you would have never seen any of that as a real possibility until you stepped through those interim worlds.

Think of the earlier example regarding the health club. Stepping through Door A involves researching the health clubs within a 20-mile radius to where you live. Door B may include speaking with health club managers and owners, and visiting a number of local clubs. Door C might be shadowing the general manager of one of the clubs. During your shadowing, a new world emerged that you didn't even know existed—Health Club Consulting and Design. With this discovery came a new set of possibilities and options (i.e., new doors). This industry existed the whole time; it just wasn't on your radar. You had to keep progressing through the doors until you discovered it. Now you can continue to play there as you figure out how to transition into this new world.

Here's another example of what I mean.

My client Dave had been in the same customer service job for years and was burnt out and ready to do something else. He had dreams he had given up on and had other ideas he found interesting, but he felt he was stuck where he was. Little by little, we got him playing in new worlds, which created new possibilities. I led him through a number of exercises (a few of which were shared with you in the *Purpose* section), which helped him define the elements he felt were important pieces of an ideal career. For Dave, these included having a lot of autonomy, continuous learning and growth, the ability to stay physically fit (he is a marathon runner), travel opportunities, and use of his interpersonal skills, along with many others. DOOR A.

We then had Dave explore some of the industries he had always been drawn to such as sports marketing and digital media sales. He conducted informational interviews, spoke with friends, and put his own personal website together as an online living resume. DOOR B.

I introduced him to some people in my own business network and he ended up doing part-time work for Scott, an acquaintance of mine, as a field sales representative for mobile ad sales. This gave Dave great new experience in sales and client relationship management. DOOR C.

This new sales experience was very attractive to the hiring manager of a software company where he was interviewing. In fact, it was this recent experience in client relationship management that led to a job offer, which he took, thus beginning his new career as a territory sales rep. He had done all of his playing while keeping his full-time day job and only gave it up at the end when he had his new opportunity. DOOR D!

This new opportunity included business travel and sales and customer relationship management; was related to the fitness industry; gave Dave plenty of flexibility in his schedule so he could continue to train for marathons; and, yes, provided him with the autonomy he craved. Back before Door A, these were simply elements of Dave's ideal career, and he had no idea that a job or industry like this even existed (therefore, to him it didn't feel possible). Yet, of course, this industry existed the whole time, and by continuing to play and explore, he was able to discover, experience, and then transition to this new world.

Ready, Set, Play!

It's time to play. Turn back to your vision from Chapter 8 and pick an area that gets you excited. Then, brainstorm three ways you might play to learn more about this area.

Which one do you want to try first? Then think it through mentally so you are sure you've made a good choice. What are you going to risk if you play in this way? For example, if you do informational interviews in your field, could you get fired from your current job? If the risk is too great, get creative and think of alternate ways you can play.

Pick the way you're going to play, schedule it on your calendar, and then go for it!

Conclusion

Play is the action that gets you from imagining to *doing*. Before you picked up this book, you probably daydreamed at least a few times about what your ideal life might look like (i.e., toyed with a vision). But have you ever played? If so, did you just barely dip your toe in the pool, or did you actually get wet? Aha! Playing *is* the difference.

Playing is experiencing. Playing is exploration. Playing is baking the bread, even if it doesn't rise or you burn it.

What would have happened if I had never gone beyond reading about coaching on my computer that first night I learned of the profession? That was safe, and that was easy, but it certainly wasn't enough to launch my coaching career. What if I hadn't talked to other coaches or gotten certified? What if I hadn't started practicing with some clients?

I would not have built a foundation that would later allow me to take the leap and fully commit to coaching, making that big transition away from the corporate mother ship to this new world I had discovered. I would not have learned about the different kinds of clients and their varied issues that I could help them with. I would not have captured the many lessons I learned from those post 9/11 years and been able to share them here with you now.

You can see how one 20-minute breakfast followed by an idea and subsequent action through play can ripple out forever. That is the power that lies inside of you right now. It may be dormant, but hopefully it's starting to wake up and come alive, scratching at the door, eagerly awaiting you to unlock it so it can come out and play.

As Satchell Page said, "Work like you don't need the money, love like you've never been hurt and dance like no one is watching." Whether you're galloping across the room yelling "nay" or dancing in the aisles, letting go of the discomfort and resistance will allow you to break through those boundaries and really play. While you may be tempted to find someone who will justify your judgments from the cheap seats, better to find another who will join you in a tango. Life-changing experiences are already out there waiting for you to bring them to life. All you need to do is play.

11

Fall Down . . . A Lot!

"If you don't fail now and again, it's a sign you're playing it safe."

~Woody Allen

A while back, my daughter, Olivia, went to her friend's birthday party at an ice skating rink. My wife, Sabrina, accompanied her there. Olivia had only skated once before with me, and Sabrina hadn't skated for years.

Olivia was initially nervous about going because she was afraid that everyone else would be better skaters and therefore wouldn't skate with her, leaving her to skate alone (although Sabrina would be there, moms and dads don't count in those situations!) But we encouraged her to just do her best and offered her all of the other so-called wisdom that parents tell their six-year-olds to get them to try new things.

Later that day, when my daughter and wife arrived home, I asked my daughter how the party was and she quickly and triumphantly declared, "It was GREAT!" I probed further, asking if the other girls had skated with her. She gave me an emphatic "YES!" She explained that after she fell down a few times, she started to get better and, by the end, she was skating faster than a lot of the other kids. I gave her a big hug.

Then I asked her how her mommy did and she laughed. She said, "Mommy skated so funny!" When I asked her what she meant, she explained, "She was afraid to fall down! So mommy skated the whole time trying not to fall down, and I told her, 'Mommy, just fall down. It doesn't hurt!' But mommy didn't want to fall down so she kept skating really funny and looked all bent over like this, and I was skating so much faster than her and . . ."

This chapter focuses on two ideas. The first is about giving yourself permission to make mistakes. Fall down six times, get up seven. Try something new and be willing to hit the ice. This is how you get better! The second idea relates to how your definition of success and failure drives your confidence, your behaviors, and ultimately your progress. By redefining these measures, you free yourself up to play without self-judgment, living your life on your terms.

Worrying about others' judgment will only cause you to be embarrassed or humiliated, which causes you to try very hard not to fall down or make mistakes. This severely stunts your learning and growth as you avoid trying new things and getting out of your comfort zone. How much freedom will you have when you combine the concept of playing and trying new things with the embrace of making mistakes and falling down along the way?

Practice Makes Perfect

When I was first starting out as a coach, I was always trying to be so perfect when coaching my clients. However, that need for perfection (really a disguised fear) was holding me back terribly. I was afraid to take chances and let my natural abilities flow because I didn't want to do anything wrong. It was completely suffocating me. It was then that my friend and mentor Fern Gorin told my class something that I will never forget. She said that people wait to do things until they have confidence. They say things like, "As soon as I get better at this, I will do it" or "I'm not ready to try it yet." But the reality is that *experience creates confidence,* not the other way around! In other words, waiting for something to be perfect is just an excuse for not getting started.

Think about that. How many things are you waiting to do, to try, or to experience because you don't have the confidence or feel that you're not "good enough?" What if you were allowed to be bad at things? Further, what if making mistakes was not only okay but was actually encouraged? I'm not referring to being reckless here. Your responsibilities still stand. However, by giving yourself a little room to stretch and reach and fall down and get up and fall down again and get up again, you will grow! That's the way it works.

So, as you read through this book and think about doing things, give yourself permission to try them and be terrible. Embrace your lousy results knowing that they are the path to understanding and learning. Allow yourself the time to develop, rather than holding yourself to some ideal state of perfection. You will gain mastery over time. But it is a process, and it takes some work, so don't beat yourself up along the way.

There is no room for critical self-judgment in this *safe space* we are creating here. In our private laboratory, you are encouraged to stretch yourself, explore, try, risk, test out, go past your comfort zone, and above all else, play. In here, we will focus on the positive growth you are achieving and the effort you've made. That means that we (you are included in "we") acknowledge the *process* more so than the *outcome.*

Learning to Fall Down

So often we stop ourselves from doing something because we fear that we won't be good at it. But remember, it's okay to fall down. Sometimes that's the only way to learn. I want you to work on playing even though you might fall down. Review and write answers to the questions below to help you let go of judgment, put away the excuses, and get out there and play.

- Where do you currently hold yourself to an extreme standard without allowing yourself time to make a mistake or grow? ("Everywhere" is not an answer—be specific.)
- What would you like to do/try/experience but haven't because you don't have the confidence that you're "good enough"?
- What happens when you don't reach this state of perfection?
- Where in your life (or business) have you given up?
- What have you used as an excuse to avoid getting started in the first place?
- Where do you make yourself miserable for the things you're not doing?
- Where are you assuming that others hold you to this same state of inflexible flawlessness?

What Is Success Anyway?

When we think about playing, we are often afraid of falling down and failing or being judged. Maybe this is because our society puts a lot of value on "success" and we worry that if we fall or mess up we will have failed. But is falling really failing, or is it learning? I argue it's the second.

Think about the Apollo 13 mission, which was supposed to be the United States' third successful attempt at landing on the moon. But it turns out that it wasn't. Due to an explosion of an oxygen tank on the spacecraft as it traveled toward the moon, the mission was aborted and the astronauts never landed. Apollo 13 was stranded in space and needed a way back home.

If the objective of this mission was a lunar landing but Apollo 13 never managed to touch the moon, was the mission a failure? Maybe. But the more important question here is this. Did the space program grow from this mission? Did the team learn? Faced with the challenge of how to get the astronauts safely home, NASA and the space crew had to dig deep and come up with a plan. They were learning on the fly, and you better believe that they all were wiser and more experienced by the time those astronauts safely landed back on Earth.

Fortunately, when you play, it will be a safe kind of play. You aren't risking life and limb; you are just exposing yourself to possible discomfort, stress, or embarrassment. That's okay! Falling down may be a little uncomfortable, but it has nothing to do with success. It has to do with the natural process of learning.

If you talk to any successful entrepreneur, they will tell you that they had to fail first—often many times—in order to succeed. By playing, you get to fail and fall down a lot because you are not putting your life or your livelihood at risk (e.g., your family's well-being, your financial stability, etc.), and you will learn a ton in the process. Playing—and playing big—really accelerates your learning curve.

If you struggle to play because you are afraid of falling down, remember we are talking about you living life on your terms. It's not about everyone else's definition of success. You are the one who determines the merits and the costs of your choices. One thing you can guarantee is that everyone will have an opinion of what you're up to. Their opinion will be cloaked in a thin veil of "I'm only looking out for you," or "Are you sure that's good for the kids?" or "Do you really want to risk what you have?"

On my small block in the Berkshires, we are surrounded by great families—salt of the earth people who would give you their last piece of bread in less than a heartbeat. I am continually inspired by their generosity and selflessness. And, yet, they are very different from one another. One, let's call him Niko, comes from Greece and is the epitome of the European male work ethic. He started working when he was very young, has little formal education, and owns a very successful restaurant. His business is his second family as Niko is always at the restaurant. He sacrifices himself, his own lifestyle, and time with his family in order to provide a better life for them. He is a true entrepreneur. He came here with one dollar in his pocket and is not afraid to take risks and strive to achieve that American Dream.

My other neighbor, let's call him John, was born and raised in our town. He works from home and is not only at all of his kids' athletic games, but he and his wife are extremely active in all of the sports leagues, the schools, and the community. Family time is paramount and they are a tight-knit crew. For John, he couldn't imagine a life like Niko's, spending so much time away from the family. Niko, on the other hand, feels that time should be spent productively, making money to support the family and a good lifestyle, not "wasting time" playing sports.

They each have different core values leading to different choices leading to different lifestyles. In both cases, they are being true to their core values, so who is right? You can come up with unlimited judgments about the benefits and costs of either lifestyle choice and that's my point.

It's easy to sit and pass judgment on what's right and wrong, but what is "right" for you is not necessarily the right choice for someone else. Don't get caught up in comparing yourself to others or someone else to you. This is about defining "success" for yourself only.

Conclusion

Do you know why children skin their knees so often? It's not just because they are still developing their gross motor skills and they're a little clumsier than us adults—it's also because they are constantly running with abandon. When you run that fast and that hard—that often—you're bound to fall down. By giving yourself permission to experiment and make mistakes, you will quickly progress from crawling to walking to running.

Use your new "letting go" muscles to release other people's definitions of success (no matter how strong or true they feel to you) and begin to identify the elements that would constitute your own definition. Remember, we're creating your life on your terms, and your definition of success and failure is going to be an enormous driver of your feelings, behaviors, interpretations, judgments, and ongoing confidence. In fact, your entire system for measuring progress will hinge on how you are defining these terms.

I hope you've started to see that the power to live an extraordinary life is within your reach. It's in *your* control. But you have to play in order to get there. You have to get out of your comfort zone and face those things that are blocking you, so you can break through them. You have to be accountable for your life, your satisfaction, your happiness, and even your direction.

That's how the concept of play leads into the next section of the book, *Plan*—where you take the learning and experience you gained through play and use this new knowledge to create the roadmap of how you are going to get from where you are to where you want to be.

PLAN

"Go confidently in the direction of your dreams.
Live the life you have imagined."
~Henry David Thoreau

12

Creating Your Roadmap

"The best way to predict the future is to create it."

~Peter F. Drucker

Now that you've played in the world of possibilities, you have a far better idea of what exists out there for you to enjoy, and which of those awesome possibilities you want to make your own. Now it's time to figure out a plan for how you're going to get there. It's time to make your vision real.

Does that news make you feel excited, scared, or both? If there is a little fear in there, that's understandable. This process will involve making a transition into a world that is still somewhat unknown and that can make us feel uncomfortable or even anxious. Hopefully, though, you are also starting to get a little excited at the prospect of creating a plan for this new life you've dreamed up for yourself. Every day, you are getting closer to living that dream.

If you find that your fear is getting the best of you, you can turn ahead to Chapter 15, "Crossing the Rickety Bridge," which is full of encouragement for taking those first steps toward your new life. Otherwise, read on and we will jump right into the work of drawing up a roadmap for how you are going to get from here to there—from your life today to the extraordinary tomorrow you have envisioned for yourself. In this chapter, we will work through breaking down your vision into parts and setting goals around each of those pieces. Action steps to accomplish those goals will complete the process, and you will then have everything you need to get from A to Z.

Let's know one thing going in, though. No matter how much you plan, the road will take unforeseen twists and turns. But, remember, you are steering the ship. When my client Adam was speaking with photographers and artists about becoming a professional photojournalist, he discovered professional retouching. He ultimately pursued that road and it led to a great job with a top NYC firm and he now does his photography on the side.

When my client Karen was pursuing her plan to become a weight-loss coach, she spoke with local gyms to see if they would sponsor her weight-loss workshop. Through those discussions, she soon discovered what being a personal trainer was really like. After playing more, she realized how much she loved personal training, and she shifted her plan to become certified in both personal training and nutrition. She currently serves as the weight-loss specialist for a great local gym franchise, delivering her combined nutrition, exercise, and weight-loss coaching program across a number of locations. Even in my journey to write this book, after countless hours of collaboration and discussion with my editor, the end result looks very different than the initial draft. Our plans are a starting point, and the ending point may look very different.

That being said, those twists and turns shouldn't stop you from putting in the time to create a good plan—because your plan doesn't need to play out perfectly for it to be helpful. In fact, the best outcome of your plan will be for it to help you manage the overwhelm of your desired change in a way that spurs you to take those first steps onto the rickety bridge of change (but more on that in Chapter 15). In the meantime, we will start by making sure that your plan is doable and realistic and can be broken down into manageable chunks. After all, how do you eat an elephant? One bite at a time.

Chunking Your Vision

If you have been willing to embrace all of the philosophies in this book so far and to design a life vision that is extraordinary, and not just *fine*, you are looking at creating some major changes in your life. The next question is . . . how do you get from here to there?

You build a viable plan.

To get started, I would like you to bring your newest version of your vision into your mind right now. This is the vision you have developed and refined as you have been learning more about your preferences and discovering new worlds when you played.

Step into a world where that vision has become your reality. Really let yourself go into this future world. Then, get as specific as you can in connecting to this future—where are you? What does it look like? Who's with you? Etc. Reconstruct a picture of this world so you feel like you're right in the middle of it. If you are going to create a plan to get to that life, you need to be engaged with what that life is going to look like.

For example, let's say you want to become a landscape designer but you are doing something very different than that right now. There's a lot for you to complete to reach that vision. The doubts, limiting beliefs, and procrastination have surfaced, but you are able to use your new anything's-possible muscles to get them out of your way. Projecting yourself two years into the future, you can see yourself having a budding Landscape Design practice that you do on the side. The business is becoming very successful, and soon you will have enough momentum to make the shift from your current work to this new career. Perfect!

Let's stop there and define that point as your goal: full-time work as a landscape designer, with income that meets your financial needs.

Now that you've got this vivid picture in your mind of the life you are heading toward, shift into planning mode. Start big by asking yourself, what are the various chunks you need to consider to get to that vision? One is the training and/or schooling you'll need. Another is the tools, software, and equipment you're going to want to use. Another area is the business setup, such as naming your company and defining the business structure (sole-proprietorship, LLC, etc.) There are more areas to consider, but essentially what we're doing is breaking down the bigger goal into these smaller chunks. That's exactly what you want to do for your own vision.

When I decided that I wanted to change my career to have my own coaching business, I followed a similar process. As with most of us, I had to devise a plan that would allow me to continue to feed my family as I made the switch over to a new profession.

How was I going to get from the corporate world to owning my own business? I still had my four-hour commute and was the sole provider for my family, which didn't leave a lot of extra time to work my action plan. Through playing, I had learned what I needed to do to become a certified coach and had put in some practice coaching hours. But I certainly wasn't fully trained yet, so there was plenty left to do to make my vision a reality. Through my initial playing, I had developed faith that my vision was what I really wanted—now it was time to figure out how the heck I was going to get there.

After procrastinating for what felt like a long time (but was really only a few weeks), I realized that trying to think of all of the moving parts at once was causing me to get stuck. So, instead, I shifted into more of a project manager mindset (I knew that MBA would come in handy one day) and started to research coaching businesses and to speak to successful coaches to identify all of the various parts needed to be completed for me to reach my vision. Identifying the various parts needed to realize my vision took some time as I didn't know all that was needed in the beginning. I didn't have to recreate the wheel. I just needed to keep playing, researching, and reaching out to the people I was meeting to develop and learn along the way.

Through my continued playing, I now knew what I had to do. For longer term plans like mine, I needed to start with longer term goals and work backward from there, breaking each goal into smaller goals and ultimately action steps.

First, I projected my gaze to the future and envisioned a time where I had a thriving coaching business. I had a pretty good sense of what that would look like because during my "play" phase, I had met with a number of coaches who had their own successful businesses and I had picked their brains.

I didn't have to know exactly how I was going to get to my vision from the start, I just needed to start with my vision and take my time as I worked backward to slowly get a handle on the different big pieces that needed to be done to get me there. A little later, I could figure out the smaller action steps that would help me accomplish those big chunks.

Let's look at how I drew up my roadmap; this will help give you a framework for doing the same. As I started to break down my vision of having a thriving coaching business, I identified the various chunks:

- develop my coaching skills
- complete my coaching certification
- create operating budgets and a business plan
- develop a marketing strategy and marketing collateral (e.g., website, business cards, a brochure etc.)
- create a legal business structure for this business
- get clients!!

There were other pieces as well, but for the sake of this example, let's limit it to what I have listed above. As you can see, thinking of all of these pieces at once can be suffocating. Can you already feel that overwhelm slowly moving in like the San Francisco fog?

That's understandable. I felt that way too. But, this time, I didn't let that feeling stop me from continuing toward my vision. Instead, I took each chunk and broke it down further.

For example, looking at just one of the pieces above—in order to complete my coaching certification, I had to find a coaching school I wanted to attend, I needed to research more about the governing body of coaching (the International Coaching Federation or ICF), and I wanted to get a few more coaching books to continue learning on my own.

From here, I set a goal around each one of these "sub-pieces" and then continued breaking them down into smaller pieces until I was left with manageable action steps that I could start with immediately. So, for me, instead of carrying the big load of "get my coaching certification," I knew I had to go to the bookstore and buy one book on coaching, register for one coaching school introductory teleclass, and visit the ICF website to learn more about certification requirements. I went from a big, overwhelming load to a small list of things that I could manage. In fact, not only could I manage them, but I was excited to begin.

Caution: Once you start moving toward your new vision, it can be tempting to disengage from your current work. But for me—and you may be in the same boat—this was not the time to check out at work. I was still getting paid a good salary and had a responsibility to the company to provide them value in return. Plus, I needed that stability as a platform to eventually jump off of. So while I was working my action steps and crafting my plan for the future, I continued to maximize my current experience at my job (see Chapter 6 for a brush-up).

It wasn't always easy—I was getting more excited as I continued down along the path to my future world, and I really wanted to simply check out at work and focus on my new direction. But that may have led to losing my current job and the foundation that came with it. If that had happened, all of my efforts would have to be spent on getting another job to meet my family's immediate needs and would have completely killed my momentum. So I knew that I had to continue to focus on my current job, while reminding myself that everything I learned, everyone I met, and every experience I had would somehow serve me in the future.

Break Your Vision Into Pieces

You try it now. Step into your vision—moving past the excuses, limiting beliefs, and obstacles—into a world where you are living that reality. Make a list of the chunks you'll need to consider to get there. These are the numerous goals and milestones you need to reach that will add up to your vision.

Take a moment to scan the list of pieces or chunks you've just identified as being important to get you to your vision. Congratulations! You are a little closer to turning today into your best tomorrow. Take a moment and enjoy this significant accomplishment. When you are ready to refine these chunks so they are realistic and doable, read on.

Be S.M.A.R.T.

Now that you have broken your vision into smaller chunks that are more manageable than the whole, I want you to tweak those pieces so you have the best chance possible of accomplishing them. You can do this by turning those chunks into SMART goals. SMART goals are those that are specific, measurable, attainable, realistic, and time-limited:

- Specific—concrete and tangible
- Measurable—how you'll know you've completed the goal
- Attainable—something you are capable of doing
- Realistic—something you can do given everything else in your life
- Time-limited—a specific date and time the goal will be accomplished by.

Examples of SMART goals include things like, "I will complete the first draft of my manuscript by October 1," "I will lose 20 pounds by November 26," and "I will spend one night each week having dinner with my family and I will limit working on weekends to a maximum of three hours per weekend starting this week."

To bring SMART goals to life a bit more, let's think back to my vision of having a thriving coaching business. I had set a goal (identified a chunk) of completing my coaching certification. To turn that into a SMART goal, I decided to rewrite it as "become certified as a life coach within the next six months."

Let's see if this goal is actually SMART. It's clear what I wanted to accomplish (specific), and I'd know that I'd accomplished it because I'd have a certification (measurable). I was certainly capable of completing it, which meant it was achievable.

Was it realistic? I needed to understand how much time and effort it would take to complete the course, and I made sure I asked questions and learned these things as I spoke with the different coaching institutes. Ultimately, I chose a program in which I was able to create the time needed to meet the certification requirements. Lastly, my goal was time-limited because it set an aim of completing the training program within six months. So you can see that my goal was indeed a SMART Goal.

Why are SMART goals so important? You'll find that SMART goals are much more motivational than non-SMART goals and that they really drive you toward the next step, which is to take these SMART goals and turn them into something you can act on. And action, after all, is just what you need to turn your vision into reality.

Get SMART

You may have already listed the manageable chunks to accomplishing your vision in the form of goals, as I did (e.g., develop coaching skills, complete coaching certification, etc.). If not, look at your chunks now and reframe them as goals. Next, tweak them a bit more to make sure they are not just goals, but SMART goals. In other words, make sure the goals you've listed are concrete rather than abstract or vague (e.g., "write two chapters by Date X" rather than "write more.") Make sure too that they can be measured by a particular deliverable. Decide on a time frame for when you will complete this goal and then make sure the goal you've set is both realistic and attainable. Are you physically able to complete it given your abilities? Do you have the necessary time and resources? If not, go back to the goal and tweak it to be SMARTer.

Planning for Action

Now that you know what manageable chunks and SMART goals will get you to your vision, you are ready to break things down even further, into *action steps*. This is where you are defining the very activities that will ultimately create small shifts in your life, bringing you closer to your ideal life.

Think about the most beautiful mosaic painting you've ever seen. Each tile on its own doesn't present the whole picture. But when placed carefully, these tiles add up to an incredible image. Think of your action steps as the tiles you are using to create your own life mosaic, one tile at a time.

When I was ready to break my goal of becoming certified for coaching in six months into action steps, I created a sub-goal to research five coaching schools to determine which one was right for me. I broke that down into even smaller action steps to make it more tangible and doable. For each of the five coaching schools, the action steps included:

- researching the program's website
- speaking with former students who were now successful coaches
- speaking with the instructors
- attending a live introductory teleclass.

I put these action steps into my calendar as tasks, spaced out in a way that was doable based on my current life and work commitments (over a four-week period). And voilà! I had gone from the intense task of getting certified as a coach to four clear action steps that would put me on the path to getting there.

I used this approach to block out all of the action steps I needed to earn my certification over a six-month time frame. For example, after

I blocked out four weeks to research schools, I added action steps for selecting which school to attend, registering for the course, and scheduling weekly study and practice time. Later in the six-month period, I added in action steps such as to draft a marketing plan for my new coaching practice and work with my assigned Buddy Coach to master the skills and exercises. In the last month, I added preparing for the coaching and oral certification exams. Using this approach of breaking my SMART goals into doable action steps, I inched my way closer and closer to my vision of becoming a coach. You can use this same approach to bring your vision to life in a realistic and manageable way.

Take Smaller Bites

Now that you've stretched yourself and have come up with SMART goals, you may be feeling a little overwhelmed by them. That's okay—in fact, it's normal. Let's take your goals and break them into action steps, which may make the whole process feel more manageable.

First break your goals down by months. What action steps do you have to do each month—for the next three months?

Next, break down each month into weeks. For Month 1, what do you have to do in each of the four weeks to reach that monthly goal? How about in Months 2 and 3? Continue to do this, defining the various action steps you'll need to take each week to get to your goals. To keep things feeling manageable, just focus on the next three months (but put a reminder on your calendar to plan out the next three-month chunk as it approaches).

Now let's set you up for success. Take out your calendar (the one you normally use, or you may want to buy one for just this purpose) and block out the times you will dedicate to each action step. This time-blocking technique is an effective way to *create* time for these tasks...since you will never just *find* time for them! Complete this process for all goals and action steps.

Doing it this way will give you a plan for what you need to do *this week* to get on your path. It will also help you see very quickly whether you've assigned yourself too much in any particular week. (Remember, the "R" in SMART stands for realistic). When that happens, reschedule your action items to work with your schedule, to ensure you will actually do them!

Once your action items are all properly scheduled, you won't have to carry around the weight of your bigger goals anymore. You can simply focus on taking the actions steps you've scheduled for a given week, one week at a time.

Conclusion

In this chapter, we've implemented a framework of breaking your vision into chunks, refining those chunks into SMART goals, and then turning those SMART goals into manageable action steps. Some of those action steps may even be broken down into smaller action steps—whatever it takes to turn your play-big vision into a step-by-step plan for making it a reality. Let's review:

Vision → SMART Goals → Action Steps

I do hope that this framework for planning will make your vision go from being a far-fetched dream to an attainable reality. But I would be lying if I didn't acknowledge that you are likely to meet some challenges and obstacles along the way. One of these challenges may be the way that you measure your success as you work toward the goals and action steps you've put into your action plan. In the next chapter, we'll talk more about the different ways to measure success and contemplate defining success in the most empowering way.

13

Setting Goals for a New Kind of Success

"Who aims at excellence will be above mediocrity; who aims at mediocrity will be far short of it."

~Burmese Proverb

When you think about creating goals, as you have just done in the previous chapter, it is highly likely that images of "success" will begin floating through your mind. Maybe it's excitement over the potential success that awaits you, or maybe it's instead fear that you will fail in accomplishing your action steps and not succeed at all.

While you are busy creating goals and enacting your action steps, I want you to pause and ask yourself how you will define success. Will you avoid creating big goals because you might fail? Will you focus on the gaps, or will you see progress when progress is made?

In this chapter, I will encourage you to explore a new definition of success that builds on the idea that it's okay to fall down (which we explored in the *Play* section). I want to free you up to not just play big, but to set big goals as you plan the path to your life vision. The bigger goals you set, the more you will be able to achieve.

"Don't Be Afraid to Make Mistakes"

In helping you to create a whole new definition of success, I'd like to start with a story . . .

One night I was sitting in a hotel lobby in New York City with a small group of friends. We were enjoying a few drinks and some interesting conversation when, all of a sudden, an older gentleman who was sitting behind us came over, put his hand on my shoulder and asked me if I was a chiropractor. While thinking that was a pretty random inquiry, I simply smiled and shared that I was a business and personal coach, which warranted a returned smile.

He told us about how he was a man who had done some coaching in his career and was a very big player in the corporate finance world—managing extremely large numbers and deals. As he put it, "a billion dollars or so—it's all the same, you just add a few zeros at the end." You could intuit from his manner and the ease in which he interacted with us that he was a very accomplished and wise soul.

He asked us to guess his age—always a trap question by people, which I try to maneuver around as best I can. But we ventured some guesses to be polite as he seemed sincere and genuinely interested. 52 . . . 60 . . . 62.

He then told us that he was 75 years old and that his youngest son was 50 and his oldest grandson was 29! He was filled with energy and spark, and we were all blown away and inspired by his presence and his essence. He offered us some tidbits of his septuagenarian mind and lastly shared the most important words of the night, words that felt like they were spoken directly to me: "Don't be afraid to make mistakes."

In fact, he said, it's all in how you define success and failure. We must make mistakes and we must fail—even if there is a little pain from it. He went on to tell us that people waste too much time trying to avoid pain and the mistakes when that is the very thing that makes us grow! A little pain is good for us, he said. Then, off he went into the night, leaving us touched, reflective, and, hopefully, a little bit wiser.

We talked about redefining success previously in the *Play* section as we discussed the benefits of falling down. Now, let's talk about how we measure our success and failure with regard to our defined goals. It's one thing to fall down when you're playing. It's quite another thing to fall down when the wins and losses actually count, isn't it?

Or is it?

Within the context of the work world, goals are concrete targets by which we are judged. Much is riding on our ability to reach or even surpass these goals. Our performance directs how quickly or slowly we progress up the ladder, it influences our compensation, and even determines whether we stay in our positions or are asked to hit the road.

Through that lens, when you set a goal, you either achieve it or fail to achieve it—a kind of binary win/lose mentality. While that has value when it comes to measuring people's performance in the world of work, when it comes to life design it is much too limiting. Let's approach it from a different perspective.

Redefining Success

For our purposes, we are going to consider a goal as a target—a place to aim for, not an ultimate ending place. With this approach in mind, you are going to use your goals to drive you forward toward your vision, but you're not going to base all of your self-judgment on whether you reach your goals or not. Yes, you are very committed to achieving those goals. You hunger for reaching them. They excite you, challenge you, and pull you forward. However, unlike in your job, we're not going to determine your raise based on the simple formula of either reaching your goals or not. In this world of life design, the *pursuit* of your goals is going to cause you to create the life you are seeking. In here, the journey is equally as important as the destination. It's not about reaching that goal at any cost; it's about making the choices and taking the actions toward those goals while considering the costs, benefits, and risks of each step along the way.

Many times we're afraid to set lofty goals for fear that we will "fail" by not achieving them. We set only safe goals and inch our way through our lives. As a result, today looks pretty much like yesterday. Tomorrow will likely look the same. We've lost our ability to dream—and then to believe that our dreams are actually possible. It seems so unrealistic that we'll ever get "there." Gentle reminder: there's no "there," in fact. Life is a process, not an outcome.

I'll give you an example from my own personal life. When my wife and I created our life plan, one of the areas we looked at setting goals around was in the area of wealth and abundance. We had to declare how much savings we wanted to shoot for that year. We had no idea because I was no longer in a job with a salary. There was nothing guaranteed, but there were no limits either. In trying to come up with a goal, however, we got really stuck!

We put down one number for savings, and we said, "No, that's not realistic" or "We'll have to work too much and not have any quality time with each other or with the kids" or "How will we do that?" We were making up all kinds of excuses for why the numbers had to be lower and more realistic so we could "achieve" them. We got stuck because we didn't know exactly *how* we would save the money.

What happens for many people when this occurs is that they don't allow themselves the room for the journey to take place. That's what was initially happening with us. We started by deciding that we wanted to save $5,000 that year, which at the time felt realistic and achievable. We felt that was a pretty doable number, well within our comfort range. Had we stayed there, we may have achieved it or we may not have. However, since we would have been shooting for a number we felt was pretty safe, we probably would have ended up right around $5,000 and felt good knowing we met our goal.

But if you think about it, we would have been completely driven by getting as close to our goal as possible in order to "succeed!" It would have become more about being right than about the path itself. By setting a safe ceiling, opportunities to save a lot more than that amount would have likely been dismissed, and we would have consciously and subconsciously driven our behavior directly toward that number. (Remember back in college how you always seemed to spend whatever you had in your pockets, whether it was five bucks or twenty-five bucks?)

We made the decision, instead, to stretch ourselves and shoot for a number that was more than we were comfortable with, having no idea how we would be able to get to it. But we still felt that somehow we might be able to pull it off even if we couldn't see *how* at that time. We committed to saving $25,000. Quite a big difference from $5,000! We agreed that for us this might be a huge stretch—we might achieve it or not achieve it—but a target of $25,000 certainly got us thinking differently regarding what we needed to do for that year. Setting a target like that forced us to get much more creative with the business and our spending and challenged us to make it happen.

Where did we end up? We actually saved $12,000 that year! That's more than double our initial goal of $5,000. Of course, we also fell far short of our goal of $25,000. So where should we focus our attention—on the shortfall (compared to our large goal) or on the extra savings (compared to our safe goal)? One perspective leads to a sense of failure, whereas the other reveals a tremendous success!

When you set high goals, you tend to shift your actions toward meeting and doing more, so why be afraid to aim high? You have nothing to lose and everything to gain.

Assess Your
Definition of Success

When it comes to defining your success *vis à vis* the goals you have set for yourself, where do you tend to focus your attention? When you set a goal to exercise three times this week and you only go twice, do you beat yourself up for missing a workout or do you acknowledge that you got to the gym twice and you'll recommit to going three times next week? Take some time now to reflect on the way that you tend to your success when it comes to working toward goals. Where do you focus your attention: on the gaps or on the positive space? When you learn to focus on your positive outcomes, regardless of whether you hit your target, you will find more motivation to keep on trying.

When it comes to designing, planning, and implementing significant life changes, the thoughts and actions you take toward that vision create the change you are seeking. So let's define failure differently: Let's say that "failure is the absence of effort, not results!"

Can you be happy with your effort even if you fall a little short? Can you use it to motivate you instead of berating yourself (which becomes another sneaky excuse to fall off of the path)? "I saved $12,000! Woohoo!" Not, "I didn't reach my goal of $25,000 so I failed."

When you are creating your plan, don't play it safe. Stretch yourself. Acknowledge your progress. The outcome and the achievement (or non-achievement) of the goal are not as important as the game itself. Take the journey that will get you closer to your desired result and enjoy the ride.

Conclusion

By redefining success and failure, you become free to strive higher. You also gain the ability to understand how to use your goals to drive you forward toward your vision and not base all of your self-judgment on whether you've reached them. You'll use your acknowledgment muscles to help you see what you've been able to accomplish along the way, not solely focusing on what's yet to be done.

With each action step you will take, you're going to move closer to living out your vision: no more "just dreaming," no more merely wishing, no more procrastinating—just pure motion toward the life that you want.

Now it's time to add a very powerful and magical ingredient that will completely determine whether you progress down your planned path or run back to your safe and comfortable old patterns. That ingredient is commitment, and it's time for you to decide if you're "all in" for making this dream a reality, one step at a time.

14

Commitment: Either Get On or Off the Bus

"It is not because things are difficult that we do not dare; it is because we do not dare that they are difficult."

~Seneca

Now that you have created a roadmap—with your vision supported by SMART goals and your SMART goals supported by action steps—you have everything you need to start creating your extraordinary life. Well, almost.

There is still one major ingredient that is very, very important. Commitment. No matter how elaborate your written plan—no matter how intricate your prescribed action steps—if you're not fully committed to your plan, it's just a piece of paper. If you want your plan to work, then you have to commit to it.

Having decided to play bigger in your life, you are now faced with a path that is no longer the easy road. Your plan will give you clear steps for how to proceed, but in undertaking those steps you are likely to bump into fears, challenges, worries, concerns, and even "failure" (although we've redefined failure as a lack of effort, not a judgment of results). How will you find the courage to stay the course? How will you avoid retreating back to your safe place—the life you have or had before, the life you are trying to shed in exchange for opening up your wings? The answer is through commitment.

In this chapter, we are going to take a closer look at what commitment is and the powerful techniques you can use to help you move from the planning stage to committed action. Commitment can come in many forms but one of the most powerful that I've found is to declare your intentions to the world. There are others too—visualization, going with the grain, reaffirming your commitment daily, and putting yourself on the hook by enlisting others' support. You can choose any or all of these techniques to help strengthen your commitment and move you from planning to action. But, first, why is commitment so important?

Commitment Explored

Commitment is an agreement you make with yourself that you are going to do whatever it takes to make your vision a reality. Commitment is going "all-in." It is the guiding force of motivation that is so strong that it keeps you engaged in the journey no matter what obstacles you are faced with. It helps you keep your vision, your values, and your behaviors in alignment, rather than allowing your behaviors to stray off course from the plan. Commitment helps you go from intention to action.

There is no such thing as being partially committed to something—you are either committed to something or you are not. A woman is not 94% pregnant; she either is or she isn't. It's the same with commitment.

When you waver, it's simple—you're not committed. When you are truly committed to something, you believe in it so strongly that you almost don't feel like you have a choice. When you have that level of commitment, you cannot be stopped in working toward your vision. You will find a way.

Think about your vision for a moment and ask yourself, is this the vision you want to commit to? Does it feel right, look right, taste right? Now return to that plan you created in the previous chapter and ask yourself if you are willing to commit to all of those action steps? It won't be easy to do all of those steps, so ask yourself—are you truly ready to commit? Is it time? Are you willing to use your muscles and sweat a little? Again, if you waver, think of the cost of not committing. Remember the reasons and the impact that pursuing this vision and taking these steps will have on your life.

Ironically, when you're not fully committed, you spend a lot of time and energy debating your commitment in your head or trying to talk yourself out of your commitment. That's what 99% commitment looks like, and that causes a lot of internal suffering. On the other hand, when you're 100% committed to something, it becomes so much easier. You summon the courage. You act in the face of fear or another emotion. You do it anyway.

Part of commitment is in the *wanting* to do something. Your passion and desire for change is great enough to pull you forward. The other piece of commitment is about simply showing up and doing what you've said you would do—being present and following through.

We've focused on the first piece—the passion—in earlier portions of the book where we gave you permission to dream and explore a new life for yourself. Hopefully, through your self-reflection and play, you have cultivated a vision that you are truly passionate about. If you have doubts, feel free to go back to the *Purpose* and *Play* sections to better refine your ideal life and work. If, however, you've got the passion piece covered and you believe that your plan is gearing you up for a life that you will love, then what's relevant to you is the part of commitment that simply involves showing up.

Imagine being a parent of young kids who need your attention on a regular basis. Are you passionate about giving them a good life and raising them well? Yep. If she skins her knee, will you go over to her? Most definitely. You're 100% committed to your child so there is no question that you are going to go and take care of her or him.

But what about those days that you are feeling tired, grumpy, or stressed by work? What about a day when you are a little under the weather or have a bad cold? On those days, your passion for parenting may be a little more muted. But your willingness to parent—to deal with a skinned knee, make the meals, run the bath, help with homework, or give a little hug—chances are, will not. That's the piece of commitment that involves not the passion but the showing up.

That's what I want you to do for your "baby"—the vision you've drawn up. I want you to commit to it by agreeing to show up. Just as you wouldn't give yourself an "out" when it comes to parenting—you would always show up when your little one skinned his knee or fell off of his bicycle or told you he was hungry—I want you to embrace a mindset of never flagging on your commitment to your plan. Can you take breaks and make adjustments? Absolutely. But what I want you to do is get yourself in the mindset that no matter what, you're going to show up.

If you're feeling overwhelmed, you're still going to show up, take a deep breath, and unbundle the mental pile that's feeling so heavy. If the day got unexpectedly busy, you're still going to show up and revisit your intended actions, adjusting them as necessary but keeping the commitment to them as a whole. If *you* fall down and skin your knee, you're going to give yourself compassion, acknowledge the effort, and get right back up and keep moving.

What does commitment look like? An example that comes to mind is what it looks like to be committed to an exercise plan. When I wake up to exercise in the morning, I have a choice about whether or not to get out of bed. But I have to tell you, when I really commit to waking up and working out, I immediately get right up and don't even allow my excuse machine to get cranking. I'm already up and reaffirming my commitment. The longer I lie in bed, the louder and more convincing my excuse machine gets, and the weaker the voice of commitment gets. So I just have to do it. I force my committed voice to yell louder than my excuse machine. "Just swing your legs over the bed," "You'll be really glad you did this," "You're NOT TIRED," "Just get up and get going," and then finally " . . . IT'S TIME!" When I'm committed to working out, being tired, cozy, warm in my bed, or sleepy won't stop me. I will feel those things, but my intention to act is stronger and so I do. I get out of bed and, off I go to the gym.

Is commitment the same thing as obligation? Am I obligated to work out? No, it's a choice. But if I am committed, I will get up and exercise.

Looking at the parenting example, some might point out that parents are legally *obligated* to take care of their children. But how many parents take good care of their kids because it's the law? Not many. Most take care of their kids because they *want* to. A commitment to good parenting really is a choice—and so is any commitment you choose to make to enact your plan for an amazing life.

It's time to either get on or off the bus. Getting on the bus is committing fully to your plan. Otherwise, don't pretend and stay in that half-committed place where you'll end up wasting a lot of time and endure needless suffering. If you feel confident that the vision and plan you have laid out for yourself is both desirable and realistic, then it's time to commit. If you are unsure, then take the time you need to reassess and make sure you're signing up for the right plan—or just commit to a piece of it to get started and then reassess a little further down the line.

If you are truly passionate about making your vision and your plan happen, you can take that passion and use it to fuel you even on days when you are tired, off, or a little grumpy. Listen to the voice of commitment that is eager to see you live out that new life you've got planned for yourself. It is that passion and that willingness to just show up, in spite of disturbances and distractions, which will keep you on track. There is one technique I use—declaring your intentions—that supports your passion and turns up the volume on your commitment. Let's take a look there.

Declaring Your Intentions to the World (and to Yourself)

When I first started on my path, I was reading all kinds of books, talking to coaches, and doing research on the Internet. I was playing, trying to get a feel for what being a coach was like and for what creating a coaching business would take.

That summer I attended a concert at the Jones Beach Theater in Long Island, NY, with my wife. During the pre-show while we were hanging out in our seats waiting for that anticipated moment of excitement when the house lights dim, I was chatting with the guy next to me. He asked me what I did in that kind of half-interested, mostly small talk kind of way, "So, what do you do?"

Normally I would answer (at that time based on my current job) something like "I do marketing for an insurance company. I help roll out technology internally to other people in the company, overseeing the training and marketing and support and blah, blah, blah . . ." Every time I heard those words come out of me, it just never felt right. I didn't want to declare myself as "that" but I continued to tell people what I did based on my job definition and list of tasks. Except that day at the concert . . .

I don't know where it came from, or what came over me, but my reply to that question that I had answered a million times before was simply "I am a life coach." My heart pounded. It felt so weird to declare that before it was true, but I had no time to engage those little demons in my head because the part of me that had been waiting so long to scream out something that finally felt right just took over. I may as well have just jumped on the stage and screamed into the microphone for the entire concert to hear, "I AM A LIFE COACH!" That's what it felt like in my two-foot block of space sitting next to some guy who had asked a very simple and common question of "What do you do?"

After I said that I was a life coach, I actually felt different—in a weird sort of limbo. I knew that I considered myself a natural coach—I would always be the one people would come to for advice, to vent, just to air things out, in confidence, etc., but I had never actually gotten paid to coach someone, so in my mind I wasn't a professional coach.

Yet, in that very instance that I declared myself to the world as a coach, something changed. I didn't know how, when, or what it would look like, but I knew it felt right and that I was indeed a life coach. It didn't even matter how the guy responded to my declaration. What was important was that I was declaring it for me and not to elicit a certain response from someone else. By the way, to my surprise he didn't look at me strangely but instead asked me what that was, and after I told him I got a big "Wow dude! That's awesome!" Not only that, he started telling the people on the other side of him (very loudly) that "Hey—this guy's a life coach. Isn't that awesome?" My wife squeezed my hand tightly and smiled. From that moment on, I was looking at the world, and the world was looking at me, through a different set of eyes, a new lens. I was a life coach. Now all I needed to do was make it real.

Another example happened with a freelance writer who was interviewing me for a story. As we got into the interview, she shared that she had always aspired to be a writer but had a full-time job and did her writing on the side. Therefore, she didn't really consider herself a writer. We got into a mini-coaching session (right in the middle of the interview!) and had her declare out loud that she was indeed a writer! We continued on with the interview and that was that, or so I thought. Here's part of the email I received a few weeks later from her:

"Mike—I interviewed you a few weeks ago for an article and I just wanted you to know that I still think about what we talked about! I have made some pretty major changes in my life (I am a writer now!) . . . I feel that the journey is right. I wrote a blog post recently inspired by some of the things we talked about."

She had indeed become a writer, and it started with her simply declaring it to be true.

Declaring your intention is an incredible technique for reinforcing your commitment to your vision and your plan and taking an idea and "trying it on for size." There's a little magic that occurs after you've done so. After you declare your intentions to the world, you can continue to commit to your plan using the techniques we're going to discuss next.

Visualize It

A key component to keeping your commitment is having a strong understanding of why you have made your commitment in the first place. Creating a clear picture of the path you are on will help you stay motivated.

Recall your vision. Where are you headed? Where are you going? How will your commitment lead you toward your vision? Everything has a benefit, a cost, and a risk associated with it. What are the benefits of honoring this commitment? What are the costs? What are the risks and how can you minimize them? What will you miss out on by not honoring this commitment?

Once you are clear on "why" you have made this commitment and why you want to honor it, it's time to visualize yourself succeeding in it. This helps keep the focus on positive success and diverts you away from the trap of focusing only on your shortfall or gaps. We used this technique (of stop focusing on the gaps) when you were defining your vision, and we also used it when you played. Now we're going to use it again to keep your commitment level strong as you move toward your vision. It's the negative focus on the gaps that triggers the fear that keeps you from taking action.

You've heard of the power of positive thinking? It's actually been proven. In fact, back in the mid-1970's, before these techniques were well-known, their introduction to the Soviet athletes enabled them to dominate the Olympics! Since then, visualizing both the process and positive results has been a key tool of athletes in all sports at all levels. In my exercise example earlier in the chapter, once I have reaffirmed my commitment to exercise and I am clear on why I have made this commitment, I close my eyes and visualize myself getting out of bed quickly and easily with no struggle. Then I picture myself going through the exercises I intend to do and feeling energized and satisfied by the end of the workout. Using this simple thirty-second visualization really makes a difference for me and helps me get right up and out of bed without suffering.

Visualization

Let's get you started building your visualization muscles. Take 3-5 minutes and close your eyes and visualize yourself following through on the action items and commitments that lay ahead of you. See yourself completing everything fully and achieving successful results with ease and confidence. Really paint a detailed picture in your mind. Write down your thoughts from your visualization: How does it feel seeing yourself doing what you said you were going to do? What blocks still remain for you to resolve? How does it affect your motivation and commitment level?

Go With the Grain

Staying with the example of waking up early to exercise three mornings per week (you can insert your own goals and commitments to them here), you are totally committed to this plan, but you know you're not a morning person. So is the plan you've created a sustainable plan? In other words, is getting up early in the morning to exercise (knowing you're not a morning person) something you think you can do consistently over the long term? Probably not. There are too many factors resisting you, including your natural rhythms. You may have good energy and strength for the first week or even longer, but over time, resistance will build and you will probably not sustain this schedule because it's not going with your natural flow. This happens a lot with New Year's Resolutions. We make a list of all of the things we want to fix about ourselves without taking into consideration the way our natural energy and rhythms flow. We may be able to succeed for the first few weeks, but like most people, by February, our resolutions are intentions of the past.

This same principle of honoring your natural rhythm and flow applies for other parts of your life as well. Are you a writer or an artist? If so, when is the most productive and creative time of day for you? Have you blocked that time as your writing or creative time? What about at work—when is your mind most productive? If it's in the morning, are you spending that highly productive time doing your intense thinking, collaborating, and creating, or are you squandering it on less-energy-intensive and more administrative and maintenance work like catching up on emails or organizing your papers? Are meetings sucking all of that high-valued time away from your day? Your most focused time, whether it's in the morning, noon, or afternoon, is when you would benefit from doing the tasks that require the most mental sharpness, like working on a proposal or speaking with clients.

It's not just about figuring out your best timing; it's also about considering your strengths and your preferences too. If you were a consultant and you were terrified of speaking in front of groups, it probably wouldn't make sense to have speaking or workshops as one of your key marketing tactics, at least not until you played, fell down a few times, and got more comfortable. Do you love writing? Create a newsletter, write articles, or write an e-book rather than have speaking as your key marketing method. When we go against our own natural preferences and flows, we create friction and use up an enormous amount of our energy resources. Typically, going against the grain ends up not being sustainable, and we have yet another reason for our excuse machine to turn on and keep us stuck where we've been. Break the pattern. Set yourself up to leverage your natural rhythms and focus your energy there.

Reaffirm Your Commitment Daily

Commitments get easier as we ritualize the activities. How much thought and energy does it take for you to brush your teeth? Not much (I hope!) By reaffirming your commitments each day, you'll be developing new habits and practices built upon your core values and desires. As time goes on, you'll do this naturally, and your commitment will become virtually effortless.

For example, each day before I leave work, I reaffirm my commitment for the next day. I review the next morning's workout and the next day's schedule, then recommit to my plan. Doing this makes my commitment have more power and makes it almost automatic when it's time to act the next day. These practices make it come alive, especially when I visualize it internally as well as declare it to someone else. Reaffirming that commitment ahead of time gives you a little more strength to combat your excuse machine when it presents you with an opportunity to bail on your commitment. When you are fully committed, there is no decision to make . . . only action to take.

Reaffirm Your
Commitment Daily!

Now it's time to build your reaffirmation muscles. Create your own success ritual to keep your commitment strong and focused. Complete the sentence:

Each day I will . . .

Ex. Review my vision and goals and the next day's action items. _____

when each night before bed

Ex. Kiss my kids before I leave for work and immediately when <u>I return home</u>

when _____

1. _____

when _____

2. _____

when _____

3. _____

when _____

4. _____

when _____

5. _____

when _____

Put Yourself "On the Hook!"

You have a better chance of keeping your commitments when you get others to support you in cementing your word. It's easy to let yourself out of something, but it's harder when someone else is holding you to account or is depending on you. For example, I had a friend who was committed to his health and figured out that the best way to get started on his exercise routine was to go running early every morning before work, before the rest of the day got away from him. He committed to his plan of getting up at 5:45 AM three mornings a week. Well, after about a week, he stopped exercising altogether; his excuse machine was just too loud that early in the morning.

So I suggested that he enroll a friend or neighbor to meet him for the run and that's just what he did. Since neither person wanted to let the other one down, they ended up both keeping their commitment knowing that the other person was there waiting for them.

You don't have to wake up before the roosters to use this technique. It can be as simple as telling a coworker what you're committing to getting done for the day or sharing with your spouse your plans for adding biking to your workout routine. Much like declaring your intentions above, there's something powerful about saying it out loud that puts you on the hook for it more than if you simply thought it in your mind. Putting it out there makes it real and gets others involved in supporting you on your quest.

Plus, when you have someone who knows what you are committed to and is supportive, you tend to keep your commitments longer. We'll talk more about this in Chapter 17. For now, make a list of the people in your life with whom you will share what you're committed to. Share with them what actions you intend to take but, just as important, why these commitments and actions are so meaningful to you.

By sharing these things out loud you will be tapping into the magic of verbal declaration and strengthening your commitment, giving you the best chance for following through on your intentions toward your desired life.

Five Tips for Committing

1. Declare your intentions to the world. Even if you feel you're not "there" yet.
2. Visualize your success, tapping into your own power and clarifying why it's important to you.
3. Go with the grain. Connect with your natural flow and set yourself up with your best chance for sustained success.
4. Reaffirm your commitment daily. As new routines strengthen, the effort required will minimize.
5. Put yourself "on the hook!" Tell your network of raving fans what you're committed to and why it's important to you and you'll find your own motivation increasing.

Conclusion

Your plan plus *commitment* equals action; your action, in turn, will lead to your desired change. That is how close you really are to creating the amazing life you have imagined for yourself.

Are you ready to commit? Are you already committed? Are you ready to take the plan you created in Chapter 12 and start working the action steps? Use the techniques in this chapter to fully commit to your plan so that when it's time to take those perilous steps toward your future, you are strong in your resilience and clear in your desire to do whatever it takes to get there.

That being said, what if you start to follow your plan and discover that you're terrified to take the first or second or third step? If that's the case, you may need a little more support to help you keep moving forward.

The process of creating your new life may feel like trying to cross one of those rickety rope bridges that spans a gigantic ravine (you know the kind—they always show them in adventure movies). It can feel scary as heck to step out onto one of those shaky wooden planks that is strung together only with rope. However, if you have a strong enough "magnet" pulling you toward the other side of the bridge, you will find the courage to move toward it. Let's explore that magnetic attraction more in the next chapter, which is designed to offer you a hand in getting across the rickety bridge by leveraging the push and pull (magnetism) of change.

15

Crossing the Rickety Bridge

"Faith is taking the first step even when you don't see the whole staircase."

~Martin Luther King, Jr.

So here you are, standing at the edge of your new life. What awaits you is . . . wonderful! It's amazing! It's incredible! After all, you've designed it! But wait. There's a whole lot of space between you and that life. You can see your new life somewhere in the distance, but you're nowhere near there yet.

Don't look down or you might get dizzy.

To use a metaphor, let's say that you are standing on a plateau overlooking a cliff. If you take a few steps out from this plateau, you will fall into the deep, dark ravine that continues down endlessly into unknown depths. You try to look down from this plateau, but doing so gets you a little disoriented. You can feel a little hint of fear creeping up inside of you, and your legs begin to tremor ever so slightly.

As all of this is going on, one thing is certain: you are going to make sure you stay right where you are. In fact, you hunker down to ensure you stay in what feels like a safe, comfortable, and familiar place.

As you peer across the deep chasm, you see a beautiful, lush, vivid, and abundant clearing on the other side. You know that is where you really want to be. However, the deep gorge that stands between where you are and where you want to be is keeping you paralyzed, locked in place.

Fortunately, there is a bridge that connects both plateaus. It has wooden planks connected at uneven distances by only rope for you to step upon and climb across. It has rope handles that are pretty loose and ever moving. The whole structure is swaying back and forth in the wind. You've been told it will hold your weight and you will be able to get across by keeping your gaze up (not looking down), and taking one step at a time, plank by plank, as you hold the rope and make your way across. However, there are no guarantees and you will have to learn as you go.

You've also been told that once you begin your passage across, it will be very difficult to come back. Oh, and did I mention that the fog has settled in thickly so you can only see a few planks ahead of you at a time? You will need a strong level of commitment to take on this challenge and begin taking those daunting steps. Welcome to the Rickety Bridge of Change.

What happens when you are just too afraid to commit and you find yourself unable to take that first or second or third step onto the rickety bridge? In this chapter, we will explore the concept of push and pull to help you understand what it will really take for you to make a change. *Push* refers to the force at your back, urging you to step onto the bridge (e.g., a job you hate, poor health, worsening relationship, boredom, restlessness, etc.), while *pull* refers to the magnet on the other side of the bridge (e.g., your compelling vision) that is drawing you to take those first scary steps toward the new life that is waiting for you. In order for you to find the courage/motivation/willpower to step onto the rickety bridge, the force of both push *and* pull need to be strong enough to get you to move.

The PUSH of Change

There are many kinds of change, but I like to think of them all as grouped into two distinct buckets: the push of change, which is reactive, and the pull of change, which is proactive.

As I've shared, the events of 9/11 served as a very powerful push for me. I felt a force at my back (a push) to move out of my current job and career into one that was more meaningful to me. In turn, it took some time for me to find my pull, graciously introduced to me by my wife's friend ("You'd make a great coach," she said innocently). Once I discovered the world of coaching and speaking, I knew there was no way I could stay running in place where I was. I now felt more than wind at my back from a job I didn't love; I also felt the pull of the coaching magnet, drawing me into my future.

Push, or reactive change, is your response to something that has already happened. You get to a point where you are either forced into action or things are extreme enough to spur you to take action. Many times, this is connected to what we'd initially consider a negative situation, even a wakeup call.

For an organization or corporation, push change might be spurred when you find your top talent walking out the door, citing a decimated culture that's been filled with bad morale, low effort and energy, and poor communications. As empty chairs replace the energy where your best people used to sit, you realize that things have to change.

For individuals, push change might look like being laid off, your husband or wife leaving you, your doctor giving you the results of the skin biopsy, or an uneasy feeling or restlessness that something has to change.

Sometimes we wait until things get bad enough to cause us to finally wake up and assess our own situation—where there are more bad days than good ones. For example, you're miserable at work and find yourself wishing away the weeks for the weekends. You're struggling mightily in your relationship. You caught a glimpse of your naked self in the mirror and wondered who that tired, old, out-of-shape stranger was that was staring back at you. Something has to change.

Yet, push change isn't always driven by a bad situation. For example, maybe you got a promotion or an unexpected job offer in another state, or perhaps your kid got into a top-ranked college.

Whether it's driven by what you'd consider a good or a bad impetus, this is what we call *push* or reactive change. In the case of a push, something happens, and then we have to deal with all of the transitions it causes. Typically, there are fears attached to it: fear of failure, fear of success, fear of being homeless and hungry, fear of running out of money, or fear of disappointing others. The list can continue on and on.

However, despite those fears, this push change makes one thing very clear: You may not know where you want to go or what it specifically looks like, but you know you can't stay where you are any longer as the costs of staying there have finally gotten too high. This is true for individuals as well as companies.

Think about being on the edge of that plateau we spoke of earlier. Without having the vision of what awaits you on the other side, and without any kind of plan to get there, that chasm looks deep, cold, and dangerous. In fact, you'll do whatever you can to stay right where you are, even when you know it's not where you want to be. (But it seems so much better than getting on that bridge, risking what you have for who-knows-what.)

Now think about being on that edge with two hands on your back pushing you forward. What is the very first thing you will do? Resist, of course. You will push back with all of your strength to ensure you stay where you are. Can you see how much energy you're using just to stay in a situation you don't even really want to be in? No wonder you're feeling hung over.

Ultimately, the push can be very helpful—it can finally get you to consider moving out from your safe hiding spot. If the push is bad enough, it will throw you out of the nest and onto that bridge. And that can end up being a very good thing.

Have you ever had an experience where at first it felt like what happened was terrible, but it ended up being a great thing over time? For example, you got laid off and the fear of unemployment was strong. Things felt bleak, prospects were low, and stress was at an all-time high. But, then, something happened and it changed. An opportunity was presented, or you met someone new, or you finally decided to try something different. Eventually you were able to look back and see that being pushed out from where you were was a good thing, even if it didn't feel like it at the time.

You may remember from an earlier book chapter how my first job out of college was working at a benefits consulting company. Great company, bad fit for me. I was fired a mere seven months later. I was living in an expensive apartment in New Jersey with a nice view of New York City . . . only now I had no income. Things were pretty dire.

One month went by, then two. I finally decided to join a local gym to do something good for myself. Within the first week, I ended up meeting a pretty girl there who I took out on a few dates. Maybe things were starting to change? Now I had a reason to clean my apartment and shower more often too! I felt some positive momentum and started climbing out of the funk I was in. Shortly thereafter, my cousin said his firm, a management consulting firm, was hiring and he introduced me to one of the Managers. Things were looking up!

A few weeks later I was hired by that company and spent the next four years doing very interesting work with great people. I was even able to live overseas in England for a year. It ended up being an incredible experience that enabled me to go back and get my MBA from NYU, one of the top business schools in the country. What was initially a terrible experience led to a chapter of my life of which I am truly proud and grateful. The push of change ultimately lead me to new opportunities and a different path.

Think back on your own life for a moment. What events have happened in the past that at first seemed bad but that somehow ended up pushing you toward something good or even great?

The PULL of Change

The other side of the coin is what I call *pull* change. Pull change can be considered a compelling vision (sound familiar?)—something that gives you a strong desire and the motivation to get to that other plateau.

Unlike push change, which causes you to move *away* from something, pull energy draws you *toward* something—because there's a vision, something compelling, that wants you to "come over here." Unlike push change, which is forcing you out of where you have been staying on this side of the bridge, pull change gives you a reason to make the trip across.

Using the rickety bridge analogy, can you see how having a very compelling vision can work in your favor and help you summon the courage to take those steps and get across the bridge? As you prepare to step onto the rickety bridge and take each action step, you are about to learn how compelling your vision really is.

Any Bugs Bunny fans here? Some of my favorite scenes when watching these cartoons were when smells came alive, as if they were actual characters. There would be a freshly baked pie downstairs, and the smell coming off of it was like a living smoke monster that wafted down the hall and up the stairs towards Bugs. When it found him, its smoke fingers would pull him by his nostrils as he floated down the stairs and across the hallway toward the pie. Bugs wasn't even touching the ground as he floated, while the aroma gently pulled him forward.

When you do it right, that's *pull* change. That's how powerful a pull can be.

If you are standing at the edge of the rickety bridge right now, realize that you will need something so strong that it will not only excite you but also pull you by the hand (or the nose) and take you across the rickety bridge, especially as those fears and doubts pop up.

Think about what your pull is. Is it the idea of working only a few hours a day? Is it discovering the "perfect" job for you or finding the love of your life? Is it driven by making a certain amount of money so you can buy that special home or have the retirement you dream of?

Now is the perfect time to revisit the vision you created in the *Purpose* section and get clear on the elements of your vision. You need to step into the dream—really see yourself there, already enjoying the fruits of the other side, that lifestyle, that work, and those choices.

If you are feeling stuck at the edge of the rickety bridge, you can tweak your vision to see if there's a way to make it more compelling to you—strong enough to draw you across that bridge. Or you can take some time to play more so you can really feel what that new life on the other side of the bridge might be like. That play experience might give you a stronger motivation to cross the rickety bridge and not turn back.

As you're doing this, note any blocks or fears that start to arise again and use the techniques you learned earlier to see how they're trying to protect you (see Chapter 4). Remember, change is uncomfortable and your blocks are trying to serve you in some way. You don't have to get everything right when you start to cross the rickety bridge; you just need to keep moving forward. Even if you are taking two steps forward and one step back, action equals success!

Conclusion

You'll need both the push and the pull to overcome inertia, uproot yourself from perceived safety, and find the strength and courage needed to move through the many blocks and obstacles that await you. You'll need the push and pull to stay connected to your passion—even when "your life" shows up. These powerful forces make sure you renew your enthusiasm and commitment to your goal and stay motivated along the journey.

What push is going to help you get out of your comfort zone? What pull will draw you forward? Tuning into those forces—and reminding yourself of why you wanted to change in the first place—may be just the trigger you need to find the courage to move across that bridge and arrive at your extraordinary life.

PERSIST

"Knowing is not enough; we must apply.
Willing is not enough; we must do."
~Johann Wolfgang von Goethe

16

Take Action Every Day

"True life is lived when tiny changes occur."

~Leo Tolstoy

Perspective, purpose, play, plan, persist. Persist! By now, you have many amazing tools in your kit to help you create your extraordinary life.

If you've been working and experimenting with the principles and steps in this book, you are well on your way toward that life. If you have been moving along at a quicker pace and plan to go back and reread the book a second time in order to work the steps, you have at least mentally moved through four of the five important phases toward creating your ideal life.

You have a sense of the importance of waking up to your life (perspective) and asking for what you want by creating a vision (purpose). You get what is meant by "play" and maybe have even caught yourself approaching life more like an experiment where you can try new things, fall down, learn, and try again. You have even created—or have the tools to create—a plan for how you will get to this new life you've started dreaming up for yourself. What's next??? It's time to get moving.

In this section of the book—Persist—we will focus on helping you move from brainstorming, intention, and planning to . . . action. The question here is—how will you get to the finish line? How will you continue to move through interruptions, distractions, your own impatience, others' resistance, and your own occasionally wavering commitment? How can you get to the place and time in which you are actually *living* your vision, not just dreaming about it?

Some of the most common blocks to getting started are the beliefs that you don't have enough time to work toward your new life and that small action steps don't count, so why bother doing anything at all? In this chapter, we will take these beliefs apart and reframe them in order to help you see that no matter how busy you are, you *can* create the time you need to make changes in your life. Then, we will examine the idea that even small action steps can make a difference, because they do.

In the next chapter (Chapter 16), we will focus on mastering the art of patience because it will take some time, and probably some courage, to make the kind of changes in your life that we are talking about. We will look at the value of sticking with the plan: being willing to do something over and over until you get comfortable and good at it. Then, you'll be ready to take on the next part of your plan and move that much closer to your big life vision.

In Chapter 17, we will explore one of the most important resources you can possibly have when working toward your life vision: your support network. The people in your life who are able to support you on your mission are key to your ability to follow all the way through on your plan to its finish. By the time you are done reading this section of the book, you will have all the tools you need to help you persist on your path to achieving your life vision.

As you know by now, the road you have decided to travel on toward an extraordinary life is not the easy one. You are going to need wherewithal, "stick-to-it-ive-ness," tenacity, chutzpah, you name it. The chapters in this section of the book will therefore round out your toolkit for life change, giving you the techniques you need to go beyond the vision and the plan—into the reality. Remember, the new life you've dreamed up for yourself is already out there waiting for you, full of promise, happiness, and good stuff. Now it's time to work the plan and stay the course. It's time to persist . . .

You'll Never Find the Time, You Must Create It

Okay, so here you are. You have an inspiring vision for how you'd really like your life to be. You've played a little in that world and you like what you see. You even have a plan for how you can get there. Not just an "I'll do it" plan, but a clear and realistic set of SMART goals and scheduled action steps so you know when and how to complete your plan.

But whoops! The first scheduled action-task date passed, and then the second, and when you look back and ask yourself why you haven't completed any action steps yet, the answer is clear and simple.

"I don't have enough time!" you say.

This is the number one excuse I hear from clients when they haven't completed an action step—they can't find the time. If this is the same dilemma you find yourself in, you are not alone in your thinking.

Note that last word there, though, because it's very important. Your *thinking*. The thought that you don't have enough time to complete your action steps is just that . . . a thought. It's a belief; not a reality.

I know what you're saying to me right now: you have tons of things going on in your life. Completely valid point. Being busy and overloaded seems to be the nature of our lives these days. I won't argue with you on that one. But what I want you to be able to discover for yourself is that no matter how busy you are, you can still *make* time to do those things that are truly important to you.

That's right, you can *make* time. This is very different from *finding* time, which, I'm sorry to say in this busy world of ours rarely ever happens. But you know what? That's okay, because you are not floating down the river any more—you are taking control of your life and being totally intentional about how you want to live it. So you really don't need to "find" time, anyway—because you are completely capable of creating it. Read on to learn how . . .

Creating time vs. making time. Let's consider a bizarre scenario to demonstrate the concept of making time versus finding time. Imagine that someone appears in your life one day and tells you with all seriousness that you need to spend thirty minutes each day this week reading comic books. At first glance, it would be easy to scoff and say how ridiculous that is. You have no time for frivolous activities such as *reading comic books*. There's no way you have time for this! As it is, you're super busy and you barely have enough time to get your work done and get home to your family each day, never mind adding this silly task to your overloaded plate.

Now, let's say that this person who told you to spend thirty minutes of your precious daily time reading comics was also a known killer and has made it clear that if you don't do as he says, he will harm you and the people you love. You have no doubt that he means what he says and he has the weapons and capacity to easily do this. Not a very comfortable thought. So, will you somehow manage to spend thirty minutes daily for the next week reading your old Archie comics? You bet you will.

So what was the difference? How can that time magically appear when it wasn't possible before? Obviously, there were different consequences attached to each decision above. In the first, there was very little upside for you to carve out time to read the comics. Therefore, it was quite easy to justify that your schedule was full and you had no time. However, when the stakes changed and there was real consequence to your decision, you figured out a way to create time for that activity. It might have meant that something else suffered. It might have meant that you had to delegate a different task to someone else. It might have even meant that you focused and worked more quickly and found a way to get everything done despite that lost thirty minutes.

See, it's not time that's the obstacle, it's you. Not having time for something may really be a reflection of:

- lack of priority
- not being committed
- not being able to say "no"
- not being focused, organized, or efficient
- having an underlying fear that's stopping you
- being overwhelmed
- not being in a good state of mind and not wanting to "deal with" the thing you don't have time for.

People often believe they don't have time. They say that they'll never "find the time" and that's the problem right there. You'll never find time; you need to create it. That means your vision has to be important enough for you to decide that it's non-negotiable and that everything else has to fit around your plan to get there.

That's one of the reasons we have spent so much time in this book making sure you create a compelling vision. Otherwise, if it wasn't a future you truly wanted to live into, it would be too easy to continually create excuses as to why you don't have the time to take the required actions to move toward it.

Are you committed to your vision? Do you really want to make it happen? Are you ready to take the small steps necessary to put it in action?

Add minutes to your clock. We're not here to wait for the perfect moment when some free time simply presents itself to you (yeah, right!) so how can you create time?

Here's my advice: Start small. Start with one small doable step! I know you're crazy busy in your life; we already talked about that. Regardless, take one of the small action steps on your plan, determine what day and time you will complete it, put it in your calendar, and just do it. Or, do it right now!

Let's look at an example of one of my clients, Daniela, who is an aspiring writer. Between her full-time job, taking care of the kids, and doing all of the things needed around the house daily, she just can't seem to find the time to write. The first thing we did was get her reconnected to the joy and passion she has for writing. We needed to make the vision of her as a writer more compelling so it acted as a pull force for change, as we just discussed in the previous chapter.

Once Daniela got excited about being a writer again, she immediately became frustrated because she didn't have the time or energy to write her book. So I invited her to start small. Finding an hour felt impossible to her so we looked at her schedule and found two opportunities where she could carve out thirty minutes to write that week. To do so, she needed to ask her husband to take the kids for those two short time slots so she could stay focused and engaged during that time. Not only did that get her writing again (she's been writing ever since and at the time of this book's publication was making great progress on her own book), but she figured out a way to increase her writing time to four hours per week. Remember, this was someone who couldn't find the time to write.

To create your own time, follow these steps and see what you can make happen . . .

- Revisit the goal you have established for yourself.

- Get clear on why it is important to you, so you prioritize it and commit to it powerfully.
- Define the initial action steps needed in pursuit of that goal or review the action steps for this goal if you've already written them.
- Take out whatever tool you use to manage your time (planner, calendar, etc.).
- Determine how much time you are willing to commit to the task this week.
- Using your calendar, block out the time and assign it to completing that task. Start with as small an increment as needed to be able to create that timeslot in your calendar—even if it's five minutes.
- Check your commitment level to complete that task. If it's not 10 out of 10, what's in the way? What do you need to get fully committed?
- Close your eyes and visualize the assigned time coming and you successfully getting into action and doing that task for the entire duration of the period.
- When the time comes, you know what to do.

Okay, it's time to make some time—and to make some progress—toward your extraordinary life.

Your Time to Create Time

When you created your roadmap in Chapter 12, you did a lot of important planning work to ensure that you were clear on what action steps needed to be done to ultimately reach your vision. Now it's time to check in. Have you begun engaging in these action steps? Or are they sitting on a pad of paper somewhere or penciled onto last month's calendar? Don't worry . . . this isn't about blame or regret. It's just a chance to assess and get going.

I'd like to invite you to go back to the action items you created in Chapter 12 now. Choose any one of them to get started. Follow the steps outlined above. For example, take out your calendar and determine when during the next week you will complete the task. Write it into your calendar as if it's the most important task on your list that day, as if harm will come to you if you don't complete it. That's the level of commitment we want from you. Just one task! Start small. Then make a plan to do that one step again and again. Small steps over time add up, until you have reached your goal.

Little Things Count

Okay, let's imagine that you have successfully "made" time. You have taken the first action step, the second action step, the third action step, and the fourth action step on your plan, and you are working diligently and excitedly toward your vision. You have energy and momentum, and your plan—and progress—are going great.

Now, stop! All of a sudden, something disrupts your action and your rhythm. For one reason or another, there is a break in your ritual. It might be welcome or unwelcome, expected or unexpected. Either way, it's really no surprise that this happened. That's life, isn't it? Eventually, something always comes up. So, let's be prepared.

How are you going to handle this inevitable break in the action when it strikes? How will you override the interruption and reinstate the flow? You need a tool to persist in your actions in spite of the break. One of my favorite tools for this purpose is using the practice of "everything counts" in order to help sustain your momentum.

Let me demonstrate "everything counts" using the handy fitness example. Let's say that you committed to go to the gym today but didn't wake up in time (break in your ritual) or something came up at work (interruption). What do you do? What action could you take to keep to your exercise commitment and still make everything work for you today?

Could you walk home from work instead? Could you do some push-ups and sit-ups at home for fifteen minutes? Can you take the stairs instead of the elevator? Can you go for a walk during lunch? Can you dance around the living room with your kids when you get home or jump on the backyard trampoline with them? What else could you do?

Are you starting to see where I'm going with this? These actions, though smaller and less impactful than a forty-five-minute visit to the gym, all count toward your exercise goal. Everything counts! Not just the big action steps but the little action steps too. Small steps build both the tangible and mental momentum needed to take you to the *next* action step and to keep you working your plan.

When you remember that everything counts, you are more able to . . .

- recognize opportunities for action and maximize small chunks of time
- sustain your momentum rather than stopping midstream
- stay in a positive mindset, learn from obstacles and interruptions, and move on.

When you run into an interruption, I want you to find something small to do—anything! Why? Because you don't want to lose your momentum; we know where that leads—to a standstill and even a backslide. And it's hard to start moving again from there.

This one small action that you take will help you progress toward your goal and keep moving forward. It may not get you to your goal today or even tomorrow, but it will keep you in motion and on track. Eventually you *will* reach your goals for the week or month, and, in time, your vision will become real.

How? You see, you are not going to just take a few small steps, you are going to take these small steps *every single day*. That's right. I want you to commit to doing something toward your life vision every single day. When you do something every day, two things happen:

1. You keep the momentum going, which is essential because the opposite of momentum is inertia and if you are standing still, you aren't getting any closer to your life vision.

2. You *make progress* toward your life vision. Each small action step means you are getting one step closer to living your dream; pretty soon these small steps add up to real change.

Everything counts—even little things. When you combine small steps with regular action over time, you will create the positive change you seek.

Take Five

Time is our most precious commodity. But these days, we have to find a way to do more with less, because it is harder and harder to find big chunks of time. That's okay, fifteen minutes—or even five—will do.

Take one of your goals from your plan (see Chapter 12) and imagine that life has interrupted your ability to work on one of your related action steps (now there's an easy task). Brainstorm three or more alternative action steps you can accomplish instead if you only have five, ten, or fifteen minutes to spend.

1.

2.

3.

Too often we discredit the value of taking a small step, and we have an all-or-nothing mindset. If we can't do something big, why do anything at all? But that's not real life.

Next time you feel an obstacle pop up, remember that with a little creativity you can come up with a small action step to keep moving forward on your plan. In this world where most of us don't have big chunks of time, life change is going to look like a lot of little things that add up.

Conclusion

In the *Plan* section of this book, you created one kick-butt roadmap for how to achieve your vision. Now it's time to work that plan through action and consistency—through persistence!

I don't expect you to always be a fireball of energy or to continue going for your vision without facing any obstacles and challenges. Not at all. You *will* get tired. You will get interrupted. You may even feel discouraged or afraid.

Expect these moments; maybe even welcome them. Learn to see them as signs that you are *in the midst* of working toward your vision. If you go to the gym and start lifting weights, will you get tired in the middle of doing your reps? Probably. If you jump on the soccer field and start sprinting toward the ball, will you eventually need a break to catch your breath? Absolutely.

What I want you to do is begin to see these moments of fatigue not as red flags to stop what you are doing—not as signals to give up or call yourself lazy. I want you to see these moments and recognize them as *part of the process*—as reminders that you are no longer on the sidelines; you are in the game. Then, open up this chapter—or go back into your mind's eye—and remind yourself of all the tools you have for persisting.

Restart with one small step and see where it leads. Then do another step and another to create the momentum you will need to get going again. By doing something small, you will keep your energy flowing in the right direction. Remember, everything counts: if you do enough small steps over time, they will eventually add up to something big. It's called your extraordinary life.

17

Master the Art of Patience

"It is better to travel well than to arrive."

~Buddha

When you look up the word *persist* in the dictionary, you will find definitions along the following lines:

- to go on resolutely or stubbornly in spite of opposition, importunity, or warning
- to be insistent in the repetition . . . of an utterance (as a question or an opinion)
- to continue to exist especially past a usual, expected, or normal time (Merriam Webster Online).

Across the board, persistence involves the idea of *continuing on in spite of outside factors* to the contrary. Although the word *patience* is never mentioned in there, it's not so far-fetched to think that patience goes well with persistence too: having patience will help you persist.

What kind of patience am I talking about here? I'm referring to patience with the plan—because it will take time to get through it all, and your plan might need some adjusting along the way. I'm also talking about patience in yourself to work the plan—because you will need time to learn, grow, and make progress. You will also need patience with the process. There is no quick fix to get you to your desired endpoint. You've got to work it, walk it, live it, own it.

That can be tiring at times, even frustrating. But once you embrace the idea that getting to your vision is a process, you may just find yourself able to have a little more patience. And the more patient you are with the process, the more you will be able to persist. What is waiting at the end of *that* rainbow? Your vision lived out in reality, of course.

In this chapter, we will explore how being patient will help you persist in working toward your vision and ultimately make it real. One kind of patience we will discuss is that of being willing to do something again and again until you get comfortable with it. Let's face it—your journey to a new life is going to involve doing many things that are unfamiliar or that stretch you out of your comfort zone. If you have the patience to stick with these new things and do them over and over, they will go from being unknown and scary to being comfortable and fine, maybe even fun!

I also want you to dig deep and find your courage. Be patient with your fears—acknowledge them—but don't let them rule you. Lastly, I am going to give you some tools for when you "blow it." What many of us call "failure"—but I call "falling down"—can easily lead you to give up and stop working the plan toward your vision. But I'm not going to let you do that. Remember, falling down is how we learn! This chapter will give you some tools for working through those falling-down moments.

If you are going to be successful in persisting toward your vision (putting energy out there) AND actually getting there, you will need to be patient. Persistence will be far more effective if there is some patience thrown in to temper all that drive and forward momentum.

Do It, and Do It Again . . . and Again . . .

So far, we've talked about engaging in consistent action on a regular basis (even with small steps) in order to keep the momentum going. But doing something again and again has another benefit too. It takes the fear away from a new action item; it softens the edge.

There is a mantra that says, "When you are afraid of doing something, do it. Then do it again and again." An incredible thing happens when you do this—you change. Sometimes you even transform. The fear goes away. It resolves. It moves from being a fear of the unknown, to a fear of the known to simply being known.

Think about the most thrilling amusement park ride you've ever seen—whether it's a crazy rollercoaster, or one of those giant slingshots that shoots you into the air. You're waiting on line to ride it for the first time, and before it's your turn, your stomach is turning, you're sweating, and your hands are clammy. You're nervous.

Then you go on the rollercoaster (or slingshot or freefall) and you survive. At the end, you are even exhilarated. For some of you, that experience is enough to get you over the fear. For others of you, you'll need to go again before you are over the fear. And maybe again.

Regardless—think of how you'll feel after you've ridden that ride ten times. Fifteen times. Twenty times. Will you get nervous right before you go? Maybe. But the fear you had before that first time will be exponentially minimized.

A few summers back, I went on a three-day solo retreat into the woods as part of an ancient rite of passage ceremony. I had never done anything like this before, but I was in the middle of a number of significant transitions, including redefining my business and exploring new places to live. I was most definitely on a life adventure and I felt this challenge would give me tremendous insight, strength, and confidence to take on the impending life changes.

I was in the woods with no food or shelter for two nights. I had nothing but water, mosquito repellent, a knife, a tarp and sleeping bag, and a whistle to blow in case I ultimately did get into some trouble or danger and needed help. My guide was holding camp a few hundred yards away, and although I couldn't see him he would have come running if he heard the whistle. I'm not sure what he would have done if a 1,200-pound bear were nibbling on me, but I tried not to think about that.

Initially, as I ventured forth into the woods, away from the safety of base camp for the first time to find a space to lay my tarp, I stopped dead in my tracks. There were these big bear-claw marks cut into a tree in front of me. A bear had used that very tree to sharpen its long claws. That got my attention to say the least. At first I didn't know what to make of it—I knew what it was but I didn't know if it represented any real threat. My mind started whirling—this was a big unknown. Was the bear nearby? How was I going to sleep here unprotected out in the open for the next two days?

But a funny thing happens when you reduce the noise, commit to your surroundings, and let go of your assumptions—things slow down and your senses sharpen. I love camping, but I've never been a survivalist or a huge outdoorsman. I don't know how to read animal tracks, and I don't know what kinds of berries are safe or which mushrooms are poisonous. My first reaction to seeing those claw marks was driven by fear of the unknown. But with the noise gone, an inner "knowing" or intuition heightened. I looked at the claw marks and saw that the tree had mostly healed. So that led me to believe that they were made a long time ago. Then I hiked all around the area and looked for bear or animal droppings (Winnie's poo, if you will.) No signs of it anywhere. So I concluded somewhat reasonably, I thought, that there were no *real* threats of big, hungry animals in the area.

Nevertheless, that first night when I was lying alone on that tarp in the darkness (there was no moon so it was pitch black), every sound felt like a threat, that is, a *perceived* threat driven by fear of the unknown.

Was it a real threat? Not necessarily. It sure felt real, though. But my earlier analysis gave me plenty of evidence that it wasn't a real or high-probability threat. Yet it still felt so real.

Throughout the night, with every noise, I jumped awake, peering out into the blackness, seeing nothing. Waiting. Then, eventually, I snuggled into my sleeping bag and closed my eyes, hoping for sleep to take me into the morning. That must have happened ten or twelve times, and then one time, I opened my eyes and there it was. The sky was beginning to lighten. I had no idea what time it was but I knew I had made it. And what happened then was astounding—the fear went away. I did it. I rode that ride. I was that guy who sleeps out in the woods with no tent. The next night, having the first night's experience behind me, I slept blissfully.

When you do something that's challenging or scary again and again and again, you move from the fear of the unknown to the fear of the known to just the known. The first night I camped without a tent, I didn't know what was dangerous out in the dark woods and I felt fear of the unknown. But the second night was beautiful because I had a better sense of what sights and sounds to expect. I engaged in the same activity but I experienced it differently.

How can you apply this premise to your life? Your work? What fears are stopping you from taking on certain challenges or tasks? What are the perceived risks of the situation? What are those outcomes that you believe are irreversible if they occur? How would that all shift after you've done it—whatever "it" is—three times? Five times? Ten times? Instead of peering into the deep, dark abyss of fear, you'd be on the other side looking back, feeling proud and strong.

Don't Forget the Courage

Doing something again and again when you are feeling fearful isn't an easy thing to accomplish. Persisting toward your vision takes the

222

patience to keep at something until it loses its uncertain qualities and becomes ritual, like brushing your teeth. Sometimes we call that *mastery*. But persistence takes something else too: courage!

Clik-clik-clik-clik-clik . . . ahhhhhhhhh! I love roller coasters. Except, it's not as much fun when your life resembles one. Or is it?

Many times we get stopped because we are afraid of "the fall" that comes with trying something new, but summoning up the courage to face those fears is how you grow. That courage will take you to the other side where you can look back and say, "That's it? That's what I was afraid of? That wasn't so bad."

I remember a few summers back, we went through that very thing with my daughter when she was faced with trying a new rollercoaster ride at the Hershey Amusement Park in Pennsylvania.

"Why are you crying?" I asked my seven-year-old. She replied with the honesty and openness that only children still possess, "Because I want to ride the Super Duper Looper rollercoaster so badly but I'm really afraid."

When we asked my daughter what about the ride was so scary, we expected her to point to the loop. But she surprised us by declaring that it was "the fall"—the first big drop after passengers did that slow, initial clik-clik-clik climb to the highest point of the ride.

She wanted to ride it so badly, but she was afraid of the fall. We tried to explain that the fall on this ride was no bigger than the other rollercoaster she had already ridden. She "knew that," but it didn't matter. That's why she was crying. Logically, she knew she could do it and wanted to try. But emotionally she was paralyzed with fear. She was feeling both a push and a pull to ride that ride.

My wife and I knew she would love that 'coaster but in our excitement for her, we unintentionally were pressuring her to make a choice before she was ready. The more we kept encouraging her and telling her how much fun she would have, the more she resisted with a plea of "I know—I want to go but I can't do it!"

Then we made a brilliant parenting move. We shut up and let her "own" the decision herself, in her own time and at her own pace. We didn't mention another word about it.

A little while later, after enjoying a few less fear-inducing rides, she told us she was ready to try it. We replied with a nonchalant "okay" and made our way toward that part of the park. She shared with us that she "saw" herself on the ride with a big smile and that made her feel okay. So, she had had her vision.

My wife and daughter made their way up toward the ride while I stayed with my younger son. My daughter had confirmed her commitment. Now came the hard part.

As my daughter and wife got to the top and were next in line, the reality of what they were about to do set in and my daughter had a sudden change of heart. She was crying and trying to drag her mom back down the stairs. When my wife got her to calm down (in a way only a mother can), they talked about it and together they decided they would try it. It wasn't until much later that I found out a promise of cotton candy played a role in this decision. Alas, my daughter had found her courage: She rode the Super Duper Looper.

When they arrived back to the bench where my son and I were anxiously awaiting them, my daughter exclaimed, "That's it? That's what I was so afraid of? That wasn't so bad. I want to do it again!" We all laughed. My daughter's boundaries had expanded as a result of her actions.

And as we excitedly went to the Great Bear Rollercoaster, we looked at our daughter and saw that she was crying again. "I want to go—I really do," she said. "But this fall is bigger than the Looper . . ."

Just like my daughter, we all will bump up against the fear of the fall as we make our way through our plan and persist to play bigger. It can be scary to try something new; it can be disorienting to face larger challenges. In those moments, find your courage wherever you can.

You might remind yourself of a time in the past when you got through something difficult. For me, I can always look back on that night I slept out in the woods.

Like my wife and my daughter, you could also plan a little reward that helps you do the right thing, even if it's for the "wrong" reason. Remember that promise of cotton candy that seemed to get my daughter over the hump? According to author and cognitive researcher Dan Ariely, we humans can be motivated by rewards that are unrelated to the primary goal.[7] What's something that would excite you enough to get you over the hump of your next challenge? Great seats to see your favorite team play? Dinner somewhere extra special? A Saturday movie marathon? A weekend get-away? Plan a reward for your efforts and see how that helps to motivate you.

Persistence is continued courage and patience to keep the effort going. The more you do something, the better you will become and the more your courage will strengthen and expand. Together with your increased will and skill, you'll be able to achieve your life vision.

When You Blow It

You see, I believe in your ability to create your life vision. I know you have the courage to do what's needed and I believe you will be able to dig down and find the patience you need to take small action steps every day—to do something again and again until it feels natural and you are able to play at the next level, biting off the next chunk of your action plan and moving that much closer to your extraordinary life.

That being said, I don't want to oversimplify things. No matter how much courage you have, no matter all your hard work and good intentions, you are going to fall down or blow it at one point or another.

Are mistakes the end of the world? If you embarrass yourself or look stupid, have you failed? Not in my book. Remember that when you fall down or "blow it," that is really just you experiencing stretch marks and growing pains. Many times you learn the most when you fall down.

No matter how hard you try or what (unrealistic) expectations you hold yourself to, you are not perfect. So what do you do then? If you are going to truly persist—and not let yourself lose motivation—then you will need to know how to handle these occasional falls. When you "blow it"—when you let your excuses and your inner voice win and you don't honor your commitment, there are three key steps you need to do to get going again:

1. Forgive yourself.
2. Recommit immediately.
3. Do something today!

If you fall, make a mistake, or really "blow it" while working toward your vision, I want you to put down the mental whip you were going to flog yourself with and, instead, forgive yourself for blowing your commitment. I know—we've already established that you're a Beat-Yourself-Up world champion! Sure, there is a benefit to that—you get to give up on your commitment. You get to stay in that familiar place of self-pity and hopelessness. But the whole point of working the plan you have created for yourself is to break those habits and get past those vicious cycles of self-reproach and sabotage.

If you beat yourself up all day about having fallen down, you won't be in the proper mindset to recommit—you'll be feeling too badly about yourself. And then the real damage will occur because then you won't feel like doing your action step the next morning or the next, and pretty soon you will have lost all of your momentum.

Once you lose that momentum, it becomes so much more difficult to get it going again because you have to start all over! Professional football coaches have what they call a five-second rule. Once you make an error or mistake, you are allowed five seconds to think and dwell on it. Then you have to let it go so it doesn't affect the next play. Give yourself a few seconds to really dwell in self-pity for "blowing it" and then forgive yourself and stop looking back.

The second thing is to recommit to your goal right there on the spot. Don't dwell on it, just recommit—and say it out loud. When you say it out loud, it makes it more real, like you're declaring it to the world and you can't wiggle out of it.

In fact, you can get yourself back on the hook if you publicly recommit to the same person you put yourself on the hook with in the first place (in the next chapter, we'll explore the details of how to put yourself on the hook). Don't worry about disappointing the other person. This is not about them. If it is about them, you may need to revisit the reason you made the commitment in the first place.

Tell your partner or friend how they can support you. You are still accountable and you still need to own your commitment, but even just declaring it out loud can help you get back on track right away.

So forgive yourself, recommit right away, and then do something that day—don't wait until the next. It is a total momentum killer. Pick up and do something today and you will put a little progress between you and your disappointment. Don't worry—you can get back on track more easily than you may think.

Let's apply these three techniques to the goal of sticking to a budget. If you blew your goal this month and just couldn't resist buying that new 3D flat screen TV on sale (I'm coming to watch the game at your house!), don't beat yourself up and say you'll start over with sticking to your budget next month. If you do that, chances are you'll really continue to blow your budget this month, putting yourself even deeper in the hole.

Instead, forgive yourself, recommit, and do something that day. Decide if the TV is really what you want. Remember, it's probably not too late to return it to the store. If you are intent on keeping it, look at how you can make it work within your quarterly budget (which may mean foregoing something next month to stay on track). Don't just ignore it!! What other things need to go? Recommit to sticking to your plan for the rest of the month; then look forward. Don't look back.

Instead of beating yourself up for mistakes or falls, why not focus instead on moving ahead to recover and get back to being your best? When you do your best, you take actions. It is through these actions that life reveals itself to you.

Conclusion

Having chosen to take the more difficult road, you will need some patience on the route to extraordinary. Can you pace yourself for the long haul? Can you dig deep and find the courage to do the things that stretch or even scare you?

When you do, something awesome will happen. The scary unknown will become the scary known; eventually, you will just be left with the known. In that moment, you will be ready to push to the *next level*. You will be ready and able to play bigger.

When playing bigger, is it possible that you will blow it? Sure. We all make mistakes, and when we play, we sometimes fall down. But, remember, that's okay—because we know that to fall down is not to fail, it is to learn. So when you feel like you blew it, go ahead and forgive yourself, recommit immediately, and do something that day toward your vision.

As you master the art of patience, you are going to master your life as well.

18

Even the Lone Ranger Had Tonto

"Alone we can do so little, together we can do so much."
~Helen Keller

What's the difference between people who successfully turn their vision into reality and those who don't? Is it wealth? Is it willpower? Is it extreme intelligence?

None of the above. The answer is . . . a support system. It's not that people who make their vision a reality are necessarily any smarter than everyone else, and they're not necessarily any stronger. It's that they have a secret ace that puts them ahead of the game: a team of people who support them, behind the scenes, in both general and targeted ways.

Consider the following statement:

"Go ask someone for support."

What feelings does that statement conjure up for you? For many of us, it brings panic, fear, defiance, apathy, and anger, among other savory emotions. For most of us, our tendency is to be the lone ranger. It's very hard to ask others for help because we equate that with weakness or vulnerability. But even the Lone Ranger had Tonto.

Those who are able to make their vision a reality understand the importance of having a support system. In order to play bigger in your life, you're going to need support, whether it's the encouragement of a spouse, a friend, a mentor, a colleague—or some combination. You're going to need tangible and practical help too, whether it's expert advice from a group of advisers if you're starting a new business, or a personal organizer who helps you build a system to prioritize and stay focused. Maybe it's a personal trainer because you decided that next year is the year that you're going to run that marathon. You've never run more than two miles at a time, but you're going to play big so you say, "Hey, you know what, that's important to me, and I'm going to do it . . . but I need help to get there."

This chapter will help you uncover many of the hidden treasures in your life—all of the people around you who can provide you with knowledge, wisdom, insight, guidance, and moral support. With this goal in mind, we'll explore a technique called "putting yourself on the hook" as a way to enlist your support team in helping you bring your vision into reality. (Once you share with someone else what it is that you are going to be doing, you are likely to feel more committed to it and sense that it is more real.) To complete the chapter, we will also look at why support teams are so valuable and will review some helpful guidelines on how to find support when you need it.

Can you grow all on your own? Sure. But the growth you will experience when you start to add other people to your team will be *huge*! Ask anyone who has ever worked with a good coach. You get accountability. Support. Motivation, and more. You just don't get a lot of those things when you are working by yourself to make life changes.

Why struggle alone when you don't have to? There are an abundant number of people around you who will be willing to support you on your way if you just ask. So go for it. Your support team will help you push your game to another level. And aren't we here to play bigger?

On or Off the Hook?

So, I have a question for you. I'm going to assume that by now you have a vision for your life and a plan to get you there. If that's true, I want to know . . . who have you told about it?

Have you put yourself on the hook yet?

We all know what it looks like when you take yourself *off* the hook. You turn down the heat on the burner and say things like, "I'll do that action step tomorrow or next week or someday." You keep your vision hidden from the rest of the world, storing it in some basement closet of your mind as if it's going to get any traction at all if you keep it all boxed up and hidden in a dark, musty, corner. Are you kidding me? No one wants to go down into that basement! Why would you stuff your vision down there? It's time to let your vision see the light of day.

Now, putting yourself *on* the hook is choosing to jump right into the kitchen and start cooking. How? You don't just start doing, you tell strategic people what it is you are starting to do. You ask for help. You make plans and ask if others will help hold you accountable. You make sure you can't just slink away from your commitments without someone else noticing. You put yourself on the hook and you don't come down until you've accomplished what you said you would.

Let's play out several scenarios to compare the outcome of going it alone versus putting yourself on the hook with others.

Scenario #1—Going It Alone at Work

You've gone to a wonderful seminar and have loads of new ideas, a fresh perspective, momentum, and great energy from the experience, which you plan to invest in a new initiative at work. Before leaving the seminar, you block off some time on your calendar to do more research on your new learning. You tell yourself with excitement that this time you are really going to apply what you learned while off-site. Then, you return home after the workshop or seminar and . . . your life shows up. Phones ring, kids scream, and work piles up. Everything is urgent and pretty soon those nice manuals you got in the seminar are fated to the dreaded "dead-book" library. When you wake up the day after the workshop, will you have the same intentions, strengths and courage that you have today? Will you keep that fire alive that is inside your belly right now and wake up and take the first step toward your intentions, no matter how small that step is? Or is the more likely scenario for you to wake up and realize that the momentum and energy you had coming out of the workshop has faded away?

Scenario #2—Going It Alone With Fitness

You create a new commitment to an exercise program. The only time you can fit it into your busy schedule is very early in the morning. You are proud of this new vision of health and well-being, and you spend the first few weeks getting up really early, even though it is still dark outside, and going to the gym. But then, you miss a morning, which becomes two mornings. Your alarm clock goes off, but it is so warm and comfortable under your covers, and it is so dark outside, that you let your mental tug-of-war go on long enough that it becomes too late to go to the gym—giving you exactly the convenient excuse you were looking for to miss yet another workout, killing any momentum you might have had left. Pretty soon your gym bag is just taking up space in the hallway waiting with longing eyes (and a few dank t-shirts) for the day you take them out to play again.

What was missing in these situations? You had a clear vision of what you wanted. You were very committed initially and took action in the beginning . . . so what happened? *You never created a support structure to help you sustain your momentum. You never bothered to put yourself on the hook.*

Let's replay those scenarios now and see how different they look when you put yourself on the hook with your support team.

Scenario #1—On the Hook at Work

You've gone to a wonderful seminar and have loads of new ideas, a fresh perspective, momentum, and great energy from the experience. You get back to your life and . . . you immediately look at your calendar and set up an appointment with your colleague to work on your new ideas. You also email your coach and tell her that you have something new you are bringing back from the seminar that you look forward to discussing with her. You've told your boss and your spouse what you're up to and have asked for their support and have even conversed about what their needs and concerns are. Together, you've come up with a plan to make it work for everyone. You've given others permission to hold you accountable and acknowledge them for all of their help. You keep taking the little steps toward your vision and pretty soon you have made tremendous strides.

Scenario #2—On the Hook With Fitness

You create a new commitment to an exercise program. The only time you can fit it into your busy schedule is very early in the morning. You are proud of this new vision of health and well-being and have found a friend who is also looking to restart his/her own exercise plan. You agree to meet three mornings per week at the gym. You spend the first few weeks getting up really early (even though it is still dark outside), going to the gym. But then, you miss a morning, which becomes two mornings. Your friend calls you up and asks you to recommit to the program, reminding you why the two of you committed to it in the first place. The next morning, your alarm clock goes off and although it is so comfortable under your covers, you swing your legs over the bed right away, before you let your mental tug-of-war get going. You meet your friend at the gym, have a great workout, and feel very satisfied that you got your momentum back. You are now back in the swing and fully committed again. You've even washed your smelly workout clothes. Good stuff.

What was the difference between the first and second set of scenarios? In the second set, you put yourself "on the hook" and created a support structure to help you keep your commitments. The result? You followed through on your commitments and made real progress toward your goals. Big difference!

One of the reasons that putting yourself on the hook works so powerfully is because you don't want to let down the other people you've committed to. Yes, it's true—sometimes we care more about letting *other people* down then letting *ourselves* down. Isn't that crazy? Maybe, but we do it, so let's stay aware. By putting yourself on the hook, you can add an extra edge of motivation to your commitment.

Of course, it's more than just not wanting to let others down. We all like to feel supported. Why not have a personal cheerleader? You deserve it. Your life vision and your happiness are worth it. Having other people rooting for your success will help you stay focused, positive, and interested.

And let's not forget that you probably don't know everything you need to know to get from here to your life vision. Let the people on your support team be a bridge of learning from here to there. They have so much to teach you if you just ask the right questions and are willing to listen.

Developing Your Support Team

When I talk about your support team, I am referring to your personal network of friends, family, coworkers, and others with whom you share an affinity of some sort or have a relationship. Your personal support team can provide different kinds of support for you. They can open new doors for you as well as feed you from their own well of wisdom and knowledge. Running through the heart of it all is encouragement and motivation to help you stay strong, focused, and committed throughout your journey.

Who can you lean on when your own commitment is wavering—when you're not at your best or when you're veering off course? It's natural to get pulled into your own day-to-day drama; your supporters can help to pull you out and regain perspective.

For me, when I'm not living my core values—not being patient, courageous, or a leader—it's really important to have someone who can shake me, break the spell, and remind me . . . hey, what are you committed to? Whether it's my wife reminding me to be patient with my kids, or my own work team helping me plan for a new talk or product, or the daily texts I get from my fitness coach encouraging me to make that day's workout, those on my own support team help me stay connected to what I am committed to.

Your support team can also provide you with objective feedback, remind you of who you've declared yourself to be, and reflect how you are showing up for other people. Those on your support team can also serve as a model for you. Ever play with the bigger kids when you were young? Learning from the models, mentors, and instructors on your support team isn't that different. By "playing with the big boys or girls," you tend to raise your own level of output.

Lastly, your supporters can provide you with access to a wealth of information and insight. There's no need to reinvent the wheel when you have a support team; instead, look around and see where you can draw knowledge and information from those who have been there before you.

What do your relationships bring to your own life? Who is on your support team, and how can you be sure to get the most of it?

Choosing your team. Well, there's no need to answer these questions randomly. Like everything else on this road to extraordinary, let's be intentional about how you will construct your team. First, let's start with the people you know; then, you can branch out and build from there.

As you collect this picture of the amazing people waiting on the sidelines to support you, you can brainstorm about how they can be most helpful to you. Over time your support team will take shape and be there to help you on your way to your life vision.

Let's start with the following exercise . . .

Brainstorm
Your Support Network

When you are ready, I want you to think for five minutes (or take out some paper and write down a list) of the following:

- people you've connected to from past jobs
- community organizations you belong to
- family and extended family members
- current friends, and friends you've lost touch with
- schools you've attended
- clubs and other organizations you currently or used to belong to.

From this list, who helps bring out the best in you? Who is a champion of yours? Who do you have a strong enough relationship with that they will "call you out" when needed? Who may have insights, information, and experience for one of the goals or chunks you've defined in your plan?

Come up with your list and then pick three people you will commit to reaching out to for support in the next week.

Once you have drawn up this list, you will have the makings of your support team right there. How does it look? You probably have more people in your network than you even realized. If not, don't worry—you may just need a little more time to uncover and remember who's in your network. Technology has made this much easier for us with applications such as LinkedIn and Facebook.

There's plenty of time, too, to network and make new connections. Think of your most social friend and who she might know that she can introduce you to. Think of your family members' coworkers, and your neighbors' connections—you don't have to have a huge contact list yourself to get connected to the right people. The people you *do* know may be able to introduce you to others if you are able to ask. Your support team is out there waiting for you . . . it's simply time to go find them.

What I really want you to do here is brainstorm about all the people in your life who have the potential to be on the team for *your* unique life vision, whether because of their experience and wisdom, their supportive nature, their particular connection to you, or something else that seems to click as being helpful. You may not know yet how it's all going to shake out—who will help you and how—and that's okay. First, I just want you to get reacquainted with all of the great resources around you.

Next, now that you've created this great list, let's look a little closer at it. Who's on your list? How long is it? How far are you casting the net? And when it comes time to actually make a move—to share your life vision or contact someone for an informational interview, for example—will you be willing to call on many of these contacts—or just a few of them? The temptation sometimes is to stay within a tight box of support made up of only close friends and family. But that can be a little limiting.

While friends and family absolutely have their place on your support team (nobody loves or cares about you more than them), they also come with a little baggage. Their opinions tend to be biased, and their outlooks not always objective. They love you after all and want the best for you . . . but it might just be *their own version* of what's best for you. Who can blame them? They only want to protect you. And let's not forget that sometimes changes in your life will affect their lives, so they may end up pushing for their own agenda instead of helping you stay true to yours. So as you start to create a picture of your support team and consider inviting people in, be sure to consider more than friends and family.

Your supporters are there to help you. You might want to ask questions of them; interview them; brainstorm with them; share ideas, plans, and visions; and just check in with them from time to time for pep talks and morale-boosting.

The question now is . . . how do you do that exactly?

Reaching out for support. Now that you've defined who may be included on your support team, it's important to know how to call upon them. When you are ready to ask someone for support, the following guidelines will help you get the most out of the relationship.

- Share *what* you're committed to.
- Share *why* it's important to you.
- Ask for the person's support—*be specific* in how the person can support you and indicate why it is so valuable to you to have his or her support.
- Get the person's explicit agreement to support you and agree specifically on expectations. *Make no assumptions!!!* This is where many misunderstandings occur.
- Set up the guidelines, making sure that you both understand that you are still responsible for your commitments and journey. The support person is there to offer moral support and encouragement, but *you own it.*

- *Don't shoot the messenger!* Talk about what to do if you don't honor your commitment. Promise to not blame your supporter for such an outcome and explain what he or she can say to you to hold you accountable without blame or judgment. It is really important that you have this conversation. Otherwise, the first time your support person reminds you of your commitment and you snap at him or her, you can say bye-bye support person.
- Acknowledge your support people. Thank them for supporting you and share what you are learning. Knowing they are making a difference and adding value for you will reinforce their support and strengthen their commitment to you.

It takes time for new learning, habits, and behaviors to become a way of life. Your support team is going to help you get there. Now that you have the tools you need to ask your team for support, you are well on your way. Well, almost. We can't forget the number one rule of support—give first.

What's the Catch?

A good support network is worth its weight in gold. That being said, there are two pitfalls I have to mention. For some people, it's all too easy to continually take from their supporters without giving anything back to them. The second pitfall is to over-rely or over-expect from their network. Let's look at each of these.

Give first. Now that we've spent some time on how your support network can help *you*, let's turn that idea on its head and consider how *you* can help your support network.

A lot of times, tips on developing your support network involve asking others for help. But what if you switched things up and made sure that the flow traveled outward from you—to those in your support network?

The first rule of networking is to give to your community first. If you keep asking and taking, pretty soon you'll find yourself alone. But, if you can join a community and start by adding value, you will have legions of people coming to you, not in a quid pro quo kind of way, but in an authentic sense of connection and conversation.

"But I'm a novice!" you say. "What can I possibly contribute?" To that, I say . . . we all have a point of view, and there is always something to offer. Take a look at the conversations that are going on in your community and share from your perspective. Sometimes it is the most inexperienced people who have the freshest set of ideas.

Delivered with humility and an open mind (this is one idea you are offering, not the only or the "right" idea), you can respectfully begin to build a bridge toward the community you are trying to create. Plus, there is no doubt in my mind that you *do* bring something valuable to the table. Even if you are moving into a new community, field, or industry, you may have years of experience elsewhere to draw upon. Trust your background and be willing to think creatively about how you can contribute to your support network. It is sure to pay dividends in terms of relationships, friendships, sharing, and connections.

Maintain ownership. Is your support network there to make decisions for you? If someone in your network provides you counsel and you make a decision based on that counsel, who owns the outcome of your decision—you or the person who counseled you?

It's very tempting to assign others your responsibilities when setting them up as a support for you. But here's the rub. Are you asking them to nag you? Are you blaming them if you still don't honor your commitments? No way! That would be doing exactly the opposite of what you are seeking—that would be taking yourself "off the hook!" That is not what we are after.

"Help me" and "support me" do not mean "do it for me," and "what do you think?" doesn't mean "give me all the answers." It's not fair to put this kind of responsibility on someone else, and I know that you really don't want to give away your power like that. Besides, you'll learn soon enough when you've overdrawn on your support network—by the fact that your friends and family start declining your requests for support.

When one of my clients was offered a job at a new company with a promotion from regional sales leader to national sales leader, he asked me if he should take the job. "Tell me," he said, "What should I do?"

So I said to him, "Rather than make a decision on the whole, let's break it down into elements. Let's look at every one of those dimensions and see what is most important to you: salary, company, career potential, impact on your life, team you'll be working with, and so on." Rather than my client using me to make his decision for him, he used me as a resource and sounding board as he explored the different elements of the decision he was making.

After completing this exercise, my client was very clear on his priorities and used them to guide his decision, which was very conscious and clearly his own. Today he's the national sales director of the company and loving his job and lifestyle.

A lot of times, we ask friends and family, "How should I handle this?" There is a temptation to find a quick answer or to want to simplify the situation or even to defer the answer to someone else. It's easier when we ask someone else to make our decisions for us; when we have to own it, it is much more challenging. Then again, the answer someone else gives may be all wrong when it comes to what we really want.

If you're relying on somebody else's advice, then you're cheating yourself of your own personal and professional growth. Sure, you may receive immediate gratification, but it's not going to develop you in the same way as if you understood the criteria and made your own decision. It also might not reward you in the same way because clearly no one knows your wishes as well as you.

Let's not forget too that you're liable to create resentment among your supporters if you over-rely on them. You may have all kinds of expectations you are placing on them that are unfair or too much, and one by one, members of your support team may decide to pull back or drop away. Or, you may even develop resentment toward them or them toward you. When you ask for something from your team, you need to be okay with what they can and can't provide for you.

Note: If you have an issue that requires professional support such as an addiction or depression, please do what you need to do to take care of yourself. You may need professional help and it is not only unwise to rely on friends and family for help in those types of situations, it is also unfair to both of you because they are not equipped to help you in that regard.

A strong support network is valuable for all kinds of reasons. The last is one of my favorites, though: connection for the sake of connection—relationships simply because they make you happy and better at what you do. Sometimes it's just nice to have other people in your life because it puts a smile on your face.

The reason that I live my life the way I do and the reason that I'm happy is almost purely because of my support network: my family, my friends, my business partners, and my clients. Connections are some of the most valuable things I can have. When I get to experience life *and* have someone included in that, it's really meaningful.

Conclusion

How is it that two people can start with the same intention and motivation, but only one actually meets the goal? Why do some people reach the vision and others don't? You know you need a plan, but that's not enough. A strong support network is essential to your ability to persist toward completion too.

When you need objective feedback in a situation, your supporters will be strong enough to provide that. When you need a little mini-wakeup call to drag you out of your drama and back toward your razor-sharp commitments, your support team can help. Even something as simple but valuable as inspiration to keep moving forward can come from the supporters in your life. A simple chat over the phone or a cup of coffee can be just the thing you need to get reignited toward action.

Never underestimate the value of your brothers and sisters to help you on your way. Not only are they there to help you persist to the finish, they can add joy and meaning to your journey.

CONCLUSION

"Life is a gift and every single day counts."
~Mike Jaffe

19

Don't Round Up, Tomorrow Starts Today

"Do it, do it I say. Whatever you want to do, do it now, there are only so many tomorrows."

~Michael Landon

What is the most important day of your life?

Stop for a moment and ask yourself. Was it your wedding? The birth of a child? The day you graduated from high school or college? Was it a religious experience you had? Most of these days are important days that revolve around big events or big actions. These are all great days—very, very good days.

It's easy to look back on milestone events and consider them the greatest and most important days of our lives. But are they? Certainly, they are ones we remember. They are experiences that we often put a lot of effort into like a wedding or party. They are outcomes we've worked hard to achieve like a graduation or a promotion. So nobody can argue that they weren't important experiences and days in the string of time that has added up to our lives. But were any of them the most important day? How do you measure that?

What about smaller experiences that unknowingly or not set your life on a new course? We can create an unlimited amount of "what if's" stringing back to our active memories. What if I had never gone to that party that night and met you? What if I hadn't woken up late that morning? What if I hadn't said yes to that opportunity in disguise?

These "smaller" experiences are important too: little decisions—tiny moments—that led to the next and then the next and then . . . suddenly your life has shifted in some monumental way. So in looking back on your life, you can find the important moments. Big or small, they are there.

Let's also consider what we talked about in Chapter 2—the storms we've gone through. Remember, we may not have enjoyed the experience, but most storms we face tend to be important mileposts in our lives. I once gave a keynote talk to a group of very successful franchise owners. As we were discussing the concept of embracing the storm, Greg raised his hand and shared how the three most important days in his life were his wedding, the birth of his child, and the day he had a heart attack. Yep, that third one was something he considered one of the best days of his life, because it woke him up to completely recreate how he was taking care of himself. He now exercises every day, eats much healthier, and deals with stress much differently than he used to. As a result, he's living a much more vibrant life, and he's likely to live longer than he would have had he not made these changes.

But what if we turned that question on its head—that question of, what is the most important day of your life? What if instead of looking back to the past (or ahead to the future), the answer was, instead, today?

Think about it. Yesterday is just a dream, and tomorrow doesn't exist. All that any of us really has is today. Today!

If we are constantly gaining meaning from our *past* without continuing to create life in the present, we are running on fuel that will eventually run empty. If, on the other hand, we are constantly operating on the idea that happiness will come sometime in the *future*, we will never get there. Why? Because we are likely to use that perspective to put off the actions today that could bring us to our hoped-for *someday*. Only by making *today* the most important day of your life can you start to make the changes needed to get to the extraordinary life you imagine for yourself.

I will do everything I can to get you to decide—before closing this book—what *one* thing you will do today so that five years from now you won't look back on today with regret but instead with the satisfaction that you made the choice to do *something*. That something will be the thing that leads to the next something and the next something, and pretty soon, you will no longer be looking to "someday when . . ."—you will actually be living your extraordinary life in the present.

In this concluding chapter of the book, we will revisit the idea of making today the most important day of your life by avoiding what I call rounding up your life. We'll look at getting rid of this "I'll do it tomorrow" syndrome because the reality is that "someday" never comes. And I don't want you to wake up some day far from now, look back on your life, and feel pain or disappointment at what might have been. All we have is today. So let's use it!

Are You Rounding Up Your Life?

Rounding up is when you have an intention ("I'm gonna find a new job!" "I'm gonna lose weight!" "I'm gonna . . .") and are ready to get started on an action step (e.g., search online job sites, start eating salads for lunch, etc.), but in the moments before you begin, you procrastinate or delay by saying, "You know what? I'll start tomorrow." You believe what you're saying at the time, you really do. But when tomorrow comes, you round up again and tell yourself you'll do it the *next day*.

Do you know what you're creating for yourself when you do that? A big pile of empty today's. Even if you manage to eat healthy or exercise (etc.) a few days in a row, a rounding up mindset will ensure that you'll lose your momentum the minute that something gets in the way. That's not living on your terms—that's rounding up!

Let me tell you a little bit more about what rounding up looks like and see if it sounds familiar.

It's Monday morning at 5:30 AM when the alarm goes off. It's the day you promised yourself you'd finally start working out again. The alarm goes "Brrng!" and you say to yourself:

"I know I said I'd work out, but it's still dark outside and it's an ungodly hour and it feels so good under the covers and I could really use an extra hour of rest. You know what? I'll start working out tomorrow. I promise I will. Really." And you hit the snooze button.

Then Tuesday morning comes and the alarm rings again at 5:30 AM. "Brrng!" Who knows why you thought you'd feel different today, but here you are once again saying the same things as yesterday. "I know, I know, I said I'd start exercising again today, but it's not a good day to get out there. I'm just too tired, and it's raining. Tomorrow for sure, I will definitely get to the gym."

Then Wednesday morning at 5:30 AM comes and "Brrng!" the alarm goes off and what do you say to yourself? "Well, nobody starts anything on a Wednesday." Then it's Thursday morning at 5:30 AM and when the alarm goes off you say the same thing again! "I know, I know I've been putting exercise off, but it's Thursday and I've got people coming in this weekend. I've got too much to do to get ready. I'll definitely start on Monday, though."

And you know what happens when Monday comes? It's the same cycle all over again, and pretty soon days become weeks and weeks become months and you still haven't started working out again. Ladies and gentlemen, congratulations, you've just rounded your life away!

Does this situation sound familiar to you?

If not the workout example, maybe it's the healthy-eating promise that you keep making to yourself. You know, the one where you're standing in line at the Party Porch Grill at Busch Stadium and you tell yourself . . .

"You know what? I know I said I would start eating healthy, but forget the salad with the dressing on the side and the club soda that I was going to order. How often am I at the ball game? I'm gonna get that grilled hotdog and a beer. And you know what, since this is my last hurrah, make it two dogs and two beers. I'll start eating healthy on Monday."

Except as it turns out, Monday is Suzy's 40th birthday and you all have cake for lunch. Tuesday, you forget to pack your lunch so you stop by your favorite burger joint for one last taste of your favorite half-pounder with fries because after today you're not going to eat fried food any more. And pretty soon it's Friday, and you shift into weekend mode, which means a few drinks, some apps, or maybe stopping to pick up a pint of ice cream on the way home to eat as you watch the DVD waiting for you by the TV.

You see? There is always some "good" reason to round your life up until tomorrow—to put off those little actions that will move you a little closer to your life vision—but you know what? There is an even better reason not to. If you keep rounding up your today's into tomorrow, you will never get to that beautiful life waiting for you on the other side of the rickety bridge. The only way you're going to get there is to take action today—action that is small, but real. Action that is consistent.

Are you ready to do that??? Consider conducting the following exercise, which really highlights the preciousness of today.

Life Is a Gift and Every Day Counts

This is an exercise someone once shared with me that rocked my world. It is designed to help you see and feel how precious today is. You can conduct it mentally, though going through the actions for real will be the most powerful.

Let's say that you have a bag of marbles, with one marble for every week you are going to be alive, and you put these marbles in a huge jar right by your bed. Every Saturday morning, you take one marble out and throw it away to show that one week of your life has passed. That's right—you throw that beautiful glass marble right into the trash. Why? Because that week is gone and you can never get it back.

If you feel good about how you spent the week—enjoying your life or making progress toward your vision—you can keep the marble instead if you wish, but it doesn't get to stay in the jar. You'll have to put it somewhere else—like in a new jar or a glass bowl or a fancy box, and this container will represent not your life left to be lived but your memories—because one week of your life has passed and, no matter what, you can never get it back.

Are you happy with how you spent it?

What is the point of losing your marbles? I want you to really see that what I am saying is true about the preciousness of today. Each and every today lived is another day spent. And we only have so many tomorrows.

Look at that jar of marbles. You get to put one marble in for each week of your life. If you are forty years old today and you live to be one hundred, you have 3,120 marbles left. Is that a lot or is it a little? Will you even live to one hundred? I hope so and you probably do too, but none of us really knows how many days we will get here on earth.

But let's not be morbid here. Let's assume you really are going to live to one hundred. You still have a finite number of days left, and each week that passes is one more marble gone from the jar. It's up to you to make sure that you are spending your marbles—your time—in a way that makes you feel good, proud, happy. The alternative is painful to imagine. None of us wants to be throwing our marbles in the trash. But if you keep waiting for someday, you're going to be rounding up your entire life, marble by marble, until it's gone.

Every day is precious. Having read this book and having reflected on the extraordinary life you want for yourself, you now have all the tools you need to start really living, today. You just have to get into action.

The Most Important Day of Your Life

What are you going to do *today* to live your extraordinary life? How will you wake up and start living? Will you discover your purpose? How can you play today, fall down, get back up again, and play some more? Or is today the day you break your goals into little action steps that craft a plan that is realistic and doable? Maybe today is the day you will persist toward your plan by taking one more step across the rickety bridge? Maybe it is the day that you will do something small (little things count!) just to make sure you keep moving forward!

We all love clean beginnings—that's why we like to start our resolutions on New Year's day. But when we keep waiting for that clean start or deferring to the next "right" new beginning, we end up rounding our lives away. Instead of taking little steps forward, we stagnate or slide backward. Pretty soon, even our intentions start to fade away as we get back into our normal routine. By the time we wake up, it could be months or years later. Years! Do you get that?

As the Human WakeUp Call, my goal and my mission is to not let that happen to you. I don't want you waking up five years from now saying, "If only I'd done a little tiny bit every day, where would I be right now?" My job is to help you follow your personal wakeup call—your moment of truth—with one small step and then another before the power of that wakeup fades away.

It's true . . . you can wait to be laid off, you can wait for a natural disaster to hit your town, or you can wait to get that look from the doctor during a routine visit that instantly throws your life onto a frightening new trajectory, or . . .

You can make a different choice. You can decide that today is that day. You can be your own wakeup call and pursue that new or different path on your own terms, because you say so.

On that path, you will look for that small step you can take and commit to it 100%, being flexible in your actions and unstoppable in your pursuit. You will create that support structure around you that you will lean on to shake you out of your own drama while encouraging you to rise up to your greatest potential. Yet, you will maintain your grip on the reigns and own your journey as your support team inspires the courage, strength, and resilience you need to cross that rickety bridge.

Isn't it time to take a hard look at your life? Isn't it time to reassess how, where, and why you're spending your time as you are—your time, which is your most valuable currency? Isn't it time to stop losing days?

You can't afford to waste your time and energy looking back and saying, "Why?" You have to look forward and say instead, "What now? Where do I want to go?" Every day brings a new beginning.

My own wakeup call came on September 10th, a day that looked like any other day. "What if I have breakfast tomorrow with my wife and daughter instead of catching the early train?" It was a simple thought, really.

But what if I had rounded up when the next day—9/11—came and I had said, "You know what? I'll have breakfast with my family another time"? If I had done that, I wouldn't be here telling my story.

Every day is September 10, 2001. On a day that looks like any other day, you can take back your life. Not someday, not next week, not tomorrow, but today. This is the most important day of your life.

It's up to you to use it.

Peace, possibility, and abundance,

~Mike Jaffe

Get Started, Today

You know that I'm not one to encourage letting time slip by. On that note, what's the one thing you're going to put yourself on the hook for *today*? What's that one thing you can do today to start your extraordinary life?

I'm talking about doing something before the night is over—make a phone call, write something down, email somebody, or block time out in your schedule so that you can really think about your vision or plan or <fill-in-the blank> tomorrow. I don't care how small the activity is. But start today. Believe me when I say that twenty minutes can make a life of difference; it did for me.

What's the one step you will take today? What's the benefit? What are you hoping to achieve? When will you take that step (define the exact date and time)? What other resources do you need to complete it? What might sabotage you? How might you get in your own way? Whose support will you enlist? How will you reward yourself? Why is it so important to take this action and make it count? What core values of yours does it support? How committed are you to taking this action? How are you going to put yourself on the hook for taking this action? Who will you share your intentions with? Now, do it! I'll wait...

A Look Back at the Five Principles

In our journey together through this book—and on this portion of your life adventure—we have covered five essential principles that you can use to shift your life from fine to extraordinary.

Perspective. An extraordinary life begins with a shift in *perspective*—a wakeup call. You may have a "small" wakeup call like I did on September 10th when I made the simple decision to take back my life and have breakfast with my wife and daughter. Or you may have a seismic wakeup call like I had on September 11th when a plane crashed into the desk where I should have been sitting on the 96th floor of the World Trade Center. Maybe your wakeup call was this book or some thought that popped into your head recently and grabbed hold of you or, instead, an event that made you look at the world differently.

To get on the road to your extraordinary life, you need to have a shift in perspective. The details of that shift, that wakeup call, will be unique to you, but the nature of that shift will remain consistent with this idea: *today is the most important day of your life*. You will realize that to get to the life you really want for yourself, you can't wait around until tomorrow; you *must* start today.

Purpose. Once you wake up to the reality that today is the day to begin creating your extraordinary life, you will have the motivation you need to start living it.

But wait a minute. What does that extraordinary life even look like? How do you want to be spending your days? What will make you feel happiest and most fulfilled? How do you want to employ your time and energy so that you will be able to put your marbles in your memory box, not the trashcan?

Each of us has a picture of what our ideal life would look like . . . that's called a vision. Each of us also has unique strengths, interests, and areas of fulfillment. What do yours look like? This is what finding your purpose is all about. Find your purpose, and you will be another step closer to living your extraordinary life.

Playing. Most of us have heard of having a vision of some sort, and most of us have heard of having a plan to get there (we'll talk about the plan in a minute). What most people don't think about, however, is a very important middle step—the third principle—which I call *play*.

Playing happens when you take an intention (hopefully related to your purpose) and turn it into an action. The goal is to discover or learn something new that will help you get closer to living your life vision in some way.

For example, if you have always wanted to be a doctor (don't worry about how old you are—remember, anything is possible), you might play by volunteering at a nearby hospital or setting up some informational interviews with local doctors. This might help you test out your theory that you want to become a physician, or maybe it will help you make connections with individuals who can write your recommendations for medical school.

When you play, you will discover new worlds and see that more is possible than you had ever thought. For example, during your informational interviews with physicians, you may learn that there are other possible paths to fulfilling your interest in working with patients in healthcare that will take less time and resources to train for. You may discover that you can consider similar options that take less schooling—like becoming a physician's assistant or a nurse practitioner.

It's in that action of playing that your life grows and starts to become extraordinary. You go from not knowing to knowing—from staying in your current situation with its limited choices to discovering new worlds and their unlimited possibilities.

Plan. Once you have played, you will be more ready than ever to make the plan for getting to your extraordinary life. It's not that all of your playing has to happen before your planning—there may be overlap and even some back-and-forth movement between planning and playing.

What is important here is that you do some playing before you launch into the be-all, end-all plan—because you might come up with a very different plan after you've played and discovered the new things that await you, which can significantly alter your plan.

Your plan is your roadmap to success, complete with SMART goals to move you toward your vision and daily, weekly, and monthly action steps to help you reach those SMART goals. Remember, SMART goals are those that are specific, measurable, actionable, realistic, and time-based.

Your plan is there to give you the "how" of moving into your vision. It tells you what actions you can take to change your life, bit by bit, from fine to extraordinary. And because your plan was created by you, it will fit with your unique vision and build on your strengths and skills. Sure, there will also be times when your plan will take you out of your comfort zone (plenty of them, in fact), but, on the flip side, your plan will also help you avoid being overwhelmed because it is made up of bite-sized tasks that you can handle a little at a time.

Your plan is an essential bridge from a life of *fine* to one that's *extraordinary*.

Persist. If you want to bring your vision fully into reality, you will need to stick with the plan for the long-term—day after day, month after month, maybe even year after year. How will you do that in the face of distraction, fears, uncertainty, interruptions, and everything else that will pop up in your way?

You now have all the tools you need to stick with the "program." You know that you will never find time; you have to make it by elbowing room into your schedule, even just five or ten or fifteen minutes a day. You will also try to do a little something every day because you know that everything counts—even the "small" stuff. When you are afraid, you will find the courage to do something anyway, knowing that it is in sync with your vision and that by doing something again and again, it will lose that edge of fear until it feels known and certain and you are ready to play at the next level. Your network of supporters will be there, too, to give you perspective, to cheer you on, and to offer you the feedback you need to stay on track.

Your extraordinary life is waiting for you, and you have everything you need to get there. Isn't that amazing?

Appendix

Life Vision Exercises

Table 1. Core Vision Questions

PILLAR	VALUES
Family: Who is important to you? (kids, siblings, in-laws, extended) Who do you want your family to be for you? Who do you want to be for them?	
Significant Other/Partner: Who is important to you? Who do you want them to be for you? Who do you want to be for them?	
Friends: Who is important to you? Who do you want them to be for you? Who do you want to be for them?	
Money: What constitutes a wealthy life for you? What is abundance? What are your basic needs vs. desires?	
Me/Self-Care/Wellness: What is important to you when you consider your health? What are your nutrition, exercise, and rest needs and wants? What is important to you when you consider your emotional well-being?	

Spirituality/Religion/Faith: What is important to you as far as spiritual practice and growth is concerned? How about mind/body/spirit connection?	
Personal Growth: What are you seeking for your personal development and growth? What is important about it to you?	
Professional Growth & Career: What is important to you in your work? What would an ideal career look like? What is important to you regarding your professional development and growth?	
Lifestyle/Balance/Fun & Leisure: What does a balanced life look like to you? What do you want to do just for fun?	
Contribution: How important is your contribution to the world? What kind do you want to make? What legacy do you want to leave?	

Table 2. Elements of My Vision for <Year>

PILLAR	Family	Significant Other	Friends	Money	Self-Care/ Wellness	Spirituality/ Religion/ Faith	Personal Growth	Career/ Prof'l Growth	Lifestyle/ Leisure	Contribution
My Vision	*KIDS* Raise happy, independent, strong, kind, thriving kids and be an active part of their lives Love them for who they are, not who I want them to be Be a coach; Be present *BRI (Wife)* Laughter, ease, partnership, acceptance, intimacy, supportive, fully self-expressed communication, shared future vision									
Annual Goals	Trip to St John for Anniversary in Oct. 1 week skiing in Berkshires with another family Asst coach for Liv's softball, Sam's baseball, football									
DAILY Elements	Kiss/hug/I Love you to the kids when I get home, before bed, in morning if I'm home									
WEEKLY Elements	Dinner as family at least 3 times/wk Help them with homework 1 outdoor activity with kids on weekend Watch kids' sports									
MONTHLY Elements	See live music 1x Dinner out w/Bri 1x 1:1 time w/each kid Get together w/1 local friend									
QTRLY Elements	Day trip with each kid									
YEARLY Elements	2 camping trips 1 beach vacation 1 romantic vacation no kids Skiing 10+days (8 with kids)									

Notes

Chapter 3

1. Art Brownstein, *Healing Back Pain Naturally: The Mind-Body Program Proven to Work* (Gallery Books, 2001).

Chapter 4

2. Noah Blumenthal, *You're Addicted to You: Why It's So Hard to Change—and What You Can Do About It* (Berrett Koehler, 2007), 53.

Chapter 6

3. From Sugailaibo Bizdo. For more information, visit www.sugailabo.com/en/

Chapter 8

4. Deepak, Chopra, *The Seven Spiritual Laws of Success* (New World Library/Amber-Allen Publishing, 1994).

Chapter 9

5. For more information, visit www.vocationvacations.com
6. For more information, visit zogsports.com

Chapter 16

7. Dan Ariely, Keynote Speech, Fifth Annual Conversation Among Masters (Asheville, NC, May 16, 2011).

Acknowledgments

"Life is the first gift, love is the second,
and understanding is the third."

~Marge Piercy

This book started as a series of individual special reports based on the audio course and ebook that are on my company website. However, we soon realized that the reports wouldn't be nearly as valuable individually as they are all together; they just didn't make as much sense alone.

That is exactly the way I feel about my life—it only makes sense, not alone, but in the context of my relationships with others. My life has been made so much more valuable and fun by the contribution, support, and influence of many, many others who have given me so much on my journey. Life just wouldn't make nearly as much sense or be as much fun without them.

As they are too many to mention all individually, I would like to provide an umbrella acknowledgement to every single person that has ever touched my life and to whom I've had the honor of knowing either directly or indirectly. Thank you for helping me become who I am.

Every single second of my life has led up to today and, although there are decisions I would make differently if the opportunity arose again in the future, I would not change a single moment, including the many storms I've faced throughout my passage. This is a particularly difficult concept to reconcile considering the direct impact the events of 9/11 had on my life and on so many of those I knew, bringing so much sadness and pain.

However, considering that I cannot change the past in reality, I view the death of my friends and so many others as the beginning of a new awareness in this world and the *birth* of my own path of inspiring others to design and live the lives they truly want. So I say to you who are no longer able to hear my words, *Thank you. I miss you.* Your spirit lives on in all of my work and in all of the many people I have been fortunate enough to work with. You continue to touch more people than you could have ever imagined and yet you will never know it directly.

There are some in my life whom I want to acknowledge specifically.

To my lost colleagues: Ginger, Stacey, Steven, Ken, Jane, Norma, Susan, Cheryl, Margaret, Maureen, and so many others, you are always in my thoughts and *you are the flame* that helps illuminate my path. Semper Unitas.

To my brilliant editor and partners at StyleMatters: Suzanne, you are *my voice.* One can only hope to have a partner like you've been. Observing a true master at work is a gift that has called me to play bigger in my own game. Seeing you take my writing and our discussions and seamlessly fill in the pieces has been truly life-changing. This book would not be what it is if not for your dedication, patience, endurance, and incredible talent. Thank you!

To my partners and peers: Noah, Tom, Theresa, Ruth, Paul, Angela, all the gals at One Lily, Alan, Betsy, Sherri, Mush, KC, Kate, Kathy, John A., Karlin, Diana, and many, many others, *you are my champions!* Thanks for keeping me motivated and focused and for teaching me how and telling me why. I love playing in the sandbox with you!

To all of my clients (former, current, and future): You are my affirmation! Thank you for your continued faith in our partnership, which allows me into your lives and behind the curtains in your businesses to do what I have been put here to do.

To my students at the Life Purpose Institute and the other organizations I have been fortunate to work with: You are my teachers and my inspiration, and I have learned so much from you all. (Don't you dare play small!)

To the Brothers' Bass: blood, no blood . . . blood! *You are my laughter and joy,* and I love you.

To all my other friends: You possess the patience and understanding to stand by me while I continue to figure out who I am. *You are my ease and fun,* and life needs a tremendous amount of both!

To my family: Beryl, Joel, Rosa, Gabe, Adam, Vanessa, Ari, Johnny, David, Janice, Max, Alex, Dietmar, Eric, Shannon, Graziella, Joseph, and the rest, *you are my foundation.* You give me the solid ground from which to build.

To my family and friends no longer here to read these words, including Poppy Mac, Poppy Louie, Gramma Sugar and Uncle Jack: *You are my spirit.* I can only hope my life impacts others as yours have mine.

To my Gram: You are my sunshine. May you continue to shine brightly and bring your delicious smile and loving ways into the world for a long, long time.

To my sister: Michele, you continue to amaze me with all of your talents, adventures, and caring. *You are my courage!* I love you very much, and I am so glad that we get to share each others' lives together.

To my parents: Mom and Dad, you are the most generous people I have ever met. *You are my freedom and my role models!* Thank you for always doing your best. What more can anyone ever ask of another? Because of who you are, I've been free to become who I am.

To my beautiful kids: Olivia and Sam, you are my hope and my smile! Seeing you grow before my eyes is a joyous miracle. I am so proud of you and love you more than I can ever express in words. Thank you for continuing to remind me not to take life so seriously.

To my wife: Sabrina, whether we are up in the mountains, in the Caribbean, or in a smelly Inn in upstate Connecticut, *you are my Home!* There is no one on earth I would rather spend time with than you.

You are my core—my heart and my soul. From the first moment I saw you on that bus in ninth grade, I knew that you were the one. Thank you for allowing me to spend my life with you, my true best friend. Because of your support, patience, encouragement, strength, and love, I can do what I do. It would not be possible any other way. Every single acknowledgement I get is yours to share. I love you.

About Mike Jaffe

As a 9/11 survivor who has transformed his life, Mike Jaffe serves as The Human WakeUp Call™ by using his own brush with tragedy as a message of self-discovery and empowerment. After a decision to have breakfast at home with his family on 9/11 saved his life, Jaffe radically changed directions in his career, leaving a secure corporate job in Manhattan and reinventing himself as a motivational speaker and professional business and personal coach.

Through his coaching and speaking work, Mike's had the honor and privilege of working with thousands of intelligent and highly creative individuals to help them transition their own lives, enabling them to shift their perspective, deepen their relationships, and create and realize the vision they have for themselves in ways they couldn't have imagined previously. He is the founder of The Mike Jaffe Company, whose programs inspire people to WakeUp their potential, dramatically increasing their business results and enhancing the quality of their lives.

Mike currently has a house in Westport, CT, lives most of the year in Great Barrington, MA, and enjoys spending time with clients in New York City.

Drop Mike a line or post a comment on one of the supportive communities below to share how you are applying the lessons from this book to your own life and join others who are waking up to the unlimited possibilities for their own lives.

Email:	wakeup@humanwakeupcall.com
Website:	www.HumanWakeUpCall.com
Linkedin:	www.linkedin.com/in/mikejaffe
Facebook:	www.facebook.com/MikeJaffeCompany
Twitter:	HumanWakeUpCall